Whitney,

Simply Radhika...

Make my recipes
your own :)

Radhika

Simply Radhika...

a traditional yet modern approach to my North Indian table

Radhika Behl

Alpharetta, GA

10 9 8 7 6 5 4 3 2   0 3 1 9 1 4

Printed in the United States of America

ISBN: 978-1-61005-469-0

Food photography: Sue Gardner
Other photography: Kate Awtrey, Sarah Meakin, Laura Noel, Anna Chen Stewart

∞ This paper meets the requirements of ANSI/NISO Z39.48-1992 (Permanence of Paper)

Sanjay, India, and Kargil...

May we gather in uncounted lifetimes and over countless mealtimes.

CONTENTS

PREFACE...

WHY WRITE THIS BOOK?

1. My children were at school. My husband was still regularly traveling with his job. I craved something more to do. A full-time job? No. I was fortunate enough to be offered a part-time teaching position, and I embraced the opportunity. Although I was eager, enthusiastic, and honored to be "Mum" and all that goes with the privilege at 3:10 p.m., something was inherently missing.

It was time for a hobby. I had casually considered pottery or painting or gardening. Mmm...not just yet. Daily Zumba classes or spinning or boot camp? Perhaps I, too, could resemble the numerous disciplined women who surround me in the carpool line five days a week? Mmm...plenty of time for that too. (Like many women of my age, or thereabouts, I have even contemplated using this free time to go under the knife and "fix" what is broken, but then I convince myself of the waste—I have no doubt that I will require "fixing" more than once. Anyway...I have an ongoing problem with my thyroid.)

Now what? Repeatedly I had toyed with the thought of creating my own recipe book—after all, I am passionate about being in the kitchen with a new or tested idea, a sauté pan, and a willing husband to impress...now the excuses I had allowed myself no longer stood ground. I had the time and the intention. I would transform my wish into a plan, then I would plan to pursue my goal; I would be free to attend to my children and with my flexible schedule still be able to binge upon a *The Bachelor*, *Top Chef*, or *Downton Abbey* marathon whenever I chose to. My vision—to be the author of my own Indian recipe book—seemed like a most doable option.

2. I want to give my children and, one day, my grandchildren something concrete to hold onto. Learning to cook Indian food is not going to happen by osmosis in our home—no grandmas, aunties, or cousins living in the same city (or country, for that matter). I had to take action. I imagine you will understand more of this nagging desire as you allow yourself to know me more.

3. I grew up in England, where eating, cooking, and buying Indian food is both extremely accessible and affordable. The UK has a large Indian population, so ethnic restaurants, ready-made meals, spices, and advice on the subject are at hand. Next to fish and chips and Sunday lunch (traditionally a roast joint of beef, chicken, lamb, or pork which is served with vegetables and gravy), chicken tikka masala (said to have originated in Great Britain) is considered to be the national dish. Yes, really. As a matter of fact, I have never met a British person who does not salivate at the suggestion of a chicken vindaloo or a lamb rogan josh. I drool equally hard in anticipation of a cod fillet—battered, deep-fried, crispy, and golden, dressed with malt vinegar and much too much salt. Mmm...a generous side of thick fries and the mirage of Daniel Craig or Arjun Rampal (Bollywood megastar—Google him, you will not be disappointed) offering me the plate would not go amiss either. Now I am digressing.

The point is that my husband and I relocated from London to Atlanta, Georgia, in 2000. My dinner parties with my new American friends became something of a novelty. Namely because many people in the Southeast (at least the majority of those I met at the time) had not previously tasted Indian food and were fast becoming intrigued by these novel flavors. This palate was fresh and daring for my guests, but Indian foods were not so readily available or written about, and people did not really know what to order if they did indeed venture into an Indian establishment. Atlanta truly boasts some wonderful restaurants with many varied cuisines...so it understandably follows then that most of the people I met in my early years in Atlanta were experimenting with popular tastes but were not particularly well versed with Indian food per se.

Unitedly, an increase in international travel, TV food channels, and cooking magazines were catalysts for a change to come about—over the next few years, friends and acquaintances were beginning to ask for and covet my recipes and suggestions. Hence, I became aware of a growing niche for something simple and informative on paper—my paper. I am not a professional chef, but I do know how to cook and serve a memorable Indian-inspired bite or two. It was time to record it.

In addition, my most cherished and "pleasingly pushy" friends continued to urge me to start teaching informal Indian cooking classes and post tips and recipes upon Facebook. Any doubts I harbored were washed away as the interest was evident. My labor of love began to evolve, and my goal proceeded to take on a definite shape.

In the interim, Atlanta opened its doors to the eateries of outstanding restaurateurs Asha Gomez and Archna Becker. Incredible Indian flavors had landed on southern soil. The faces of Anjum Anand, Sanjeev Kapoor, Vikas Khanna, Maneet Chauhan, and Atul Kochhar (to name only a few) were simultaneously appearing in the global arena of Indian cuisine.

The above reasons were justification enough to put pen to paper, but most of all, the image of being able to cup my head in both hands and exclaim, "Let me be, I have writer's block!" whenever my husband asked what I had done all day, thrilled me to no end.

Atlanta
USA

Newcastle
ENGLAND

New Delhi
INDIA

WHO IS THIS BOOK FOR?

1.   Me. I am like anyone else who occasionally, and sometimes regularly, finds herself falling into the rut of doling out the same meals time and time again. Certainly, my family has its favorites and those recipes that I can whip up with my eyes closed, but sometimes I want to put forth a "wow" dinner for no apparent reason. What though? When picking up an inviting cookbook or food magazine, I am almost always reminded of something scrumptious that I have prepared or tasted in the past and is now forgotten or am intrigued to realize that a seemingly difficult recipe is not quite the battle I had it pictured to be. There is something about being able to physically tiptoe over that enticing photograph with your very own fingers that makes the dish seem far more accessible than not. My catalogue will arm me with an optional departure from our norm. Unmistakably, it is because of the variety (or the "departure") at our dining table that the "favorites" have become just those.

2.   Actually, I envisage most anyone being able to learn and create something, however small, from my recipes. This someone may well be a beginner in the kitchen and might have no or little knowledge of the tastes they are about to conjure up. My notion is that the dishes I write about are achievable by ALL— even by those who have only eaten Indian food in restaurants or in the homes of friends or by those who have heard about the craze but have not yet had the opportunity nor the inclination to taste or emulate it. Here is their chance. I am drawing the starting line.

3.   Even knowledgeable meal-makers can glean something from someone else's idea. I know that I comprehend something of the North Indian cooking style, yet I have absolutely no shame in adopting others' suggestions to mimic at my next table. I emphasize that I am not condoning taking someone else's recipe and promoting it as one's own—I am speaking of understanding how to lay the table, scoping how to serve finger foods at a large gathering, and noting how many sides are truly required when you extend an invitation to dinner. The way in which you choose to host should be an amalgamation of all the positive impressions you have experienced at a formal event, a mums' coffee morning, or even a simple recipe book— mine. I imagine that someone who is fairly confident with Indian spices and techniques may gather an idea or two from me in much the same way that I do while reading a friend's, auntie's, or celebrity chef's Indian recipe.

4.   It is impossible to forget the young Indian reader who has not the time nor the desire to spend hours fostering the details of nursing a dish in the way our mothers and grandmothers still do (I am speaking of myself and my multiple friends of Indian origin— second- and third-generation Indians outside the "homeland"). I know that nothing satisfies my taste buds in the same way as my mum's delicacies, but if I am to successfully pass on these unique tastes, aromas, spices, and the family history of these plates to my children, I became astutely aware that I was going to have to make things less complicated. I am certain that no Indian grandmother would ever admit to cutting corners, but I am just as confident that their daughters and daughters-in-law were brave enough to consider it. I am even further removed—the granddaughter—so here goes...

I need to note that simplifying the recipes is not meant to detract from the authenticity of the dish, nor do I believe that it does. I am not attempting to "westernize" the dishes (although you will come across some fusion ideas as you read on), but I am going to show you the way in which many Indians, including my own family in England, India, and the US, are eating at home today.

My intent is that this book will also be used by those who already truly take pleasure in making something magical happen in the kitchen or at the kitchen table (we are talking about food here). I am referring to the artist for whom creating a meal—whether it be a one-pot supper or a four-course feast—can afford an enormous amount of satisfaction. It certainly does that for myself. I swell with pride and am internally glowing when I see my friends reach for a second serving or when my daughter says that someone else's chickpeas do not taste quite like her mummy's or when my husband chooses to ignore his iPhone ringing so that he may continue to rewardingly consume his meal (okay, the latter has not yet happened). It is all about giving your time, patience, and choices and then combining them to make someone else feel the same pleasure that you are endowing. Now, this does not happen every night in our home but it *does* happen—more often than not. It is about conveying that same feeling with others. I will forever remember my son, while being interviewed for a place at a new school, telling the Director of Admissions that his favorite meal is rice and "dal" (lentils). She had never heard of it, so he offered to bring in some of the same if he ever came back. He returned that August with a heavy backpack and a date to carry in the gift of lunch. She understood that Kargil had wanted to share something that felt secure and comforting to him. She gladly received it. They made a connection—a communication.

I am sure that the sentiments are similar when someone carves out the time to cook dinner for you? I am the first to visit a written-up restaurant, but when a friend invites me into his home to share in something that was prepared for us all, I am immersed in something much more—a marked pouring of generosity. This person is investing in our relationship. I am not speaking of a lavish extravaganza, but a hearty pasta dinner, an indulgent bacon and waffle breakfast, or a southern BBQ—they all perfectly fit my bill.

The spirit of my book is, in essence, to show you how easily you can arouse those smiles and connections at your table via Indian food.

Now, you may be one of those meal-makers who considers it a chore to decide upon which vegetable to dice or ponders over who is going to wash the pan if you actually use it...well, if you can get over these hurdles and decide that you *are* going to put a healthy, homemade, mouth-watering option in front of yourself and others, then read on because this book will show you how simple it can be to do it the Indian way.

If the pull to cook is still not stirring just lay this book on your coffee table. If collectors can amass soap bars or celebrity locks of hair...then I see no problem with a growing pile of handsome recipe books.

WHY COOK INDIAN FOOD?

1. It is a cuisine that can be personalized. There are seemingly infinite variations on a dish (e.g., the level of spice and your choice of produce) and therefore such an array of plates that can be created that there is sure to be something to please all.

2. It can truly satisfy non-vegetarian, vegetarian, and vegan requirements with equal ease. In addition, I am not an expert on food allergies, but I do know that Indian food is often a wise choice for my gluten-free-eating friends.

3. It is simpler to cook than one imagines. That is the truth. It is not the creation of the meal that has to be complex, it is the flavors within the dish that are, and once you have risked the new spices or recipes a few times, you will be executing your Indian dishes with authority—oh and it will be far less painful than mastering the art of pleating, pinning, and perfecting your sari! Furthermore, I do not own any fancy kitchen appliances as no high-tech utensils are required—yes, they can surely simplify or quicken a task, but other than a food processor, a blender, and a grinder (all of which I rarely use, for contempt of having to wash, dry, and put away those intricate parts), I utilize what anyone with a basic kitchen already possesses.

4. Research has shown that the ingredients traditionally used in Indian cooking offer innumerable health benefits—you only have to listen to one of America's favorite doctors, Dr. Oz, rave about the advantages of including turmeric in the diet (see section on "Spices and Herbs"); nowadays, it is even appearing as an ingredient in some ever-so-trendy cocktail bars. However, there is a misconception that Indian food has to be spicy—not true. Granted, many spices are used but *you* are able to decide upon the level of inclusion. Let us do as TV chefs suggest—throw out the idea to "invade" and subtly opt to "pervade" your dish. It is the unique flavors that spices add to the meal (and not just the heat element) that gives Indian food its distinctive qualities. Furthermore, these spices are now available in many grocery stores, specialty/ethnic stores, farmers' markets, and online. It used to be that other staples of the Indian diet (e.g. "chapattis"/"naan" (breads), "paneer" (cheese), "garam masala" (a blend of spices), and plain yogurt) had to be homemade but now they are customer-ready and waiting to be purchased in many regular stores. There is nothing to stop you.

5. If you cook Indian food at home (as opposed to only opting to eating it in an Indian restaurant) it is more probable that you can allow yourself to serve a more healthy and well-balanced option. Limiting the amount of oil used in a recipe and using a moderate amount of grains, beans, vegetables, and protein cannot be a bad thing.

What we eat in restaurants is often memorable and at its best something that you want to revisit again and again, but if you tweak the ingredients slightly, you really can eat more of it and more often—I am learning this too...then I forget it and then I re-learn it...you might appreciate the tale.

6. It is as easy to make a dish for two as it is to prepare it for ten or twelve guests. Indians are generally known to have an "open door" philosophy where anyone and their friends are welcome at the table. My grandmother, and later my mum, always feared that an "unexpected" visitor would land at our home and there might not be something substantial to offer the guest. To be honest, there was habitually more than enough to go around and the only "unexpected" was if no one showed up.

There is the old adage that the non-Indian hostess believes there was enough food at her dinner when the serving platters are empty at the end of the night—everyone clearly devoured the meal. On the other hand, the Indian hostess only knows her party to be a success when there are enough leftovers to feed the party again—everyone (as expected) clearly devoured the meal, ate as much as they could, and—even with the temptation of more scrumptiousness—could not possibly consume another bite! It is all about abundance in the Punjabi kitchen—loud and liberal abundance at that. For this reason, there is usually a larger pot than is necessary bubbling at the stove. It does not really add too much extra time to the cooking process, only a little at the prepping stage.

The real advantage in today's busy world is that many recipes can be cooked in larger quantities and then frozen in the desired portion size. You will see which recipes are freezer-friendly (*) while reading on.

7.   It is perfect for entertaining. I am totally comfortable if cooking an Indian meal for twenty friends, but ask my husband what state I am in when Christmas lunch has to reach the table. Let me share with you that the consumption of my preferred Cabernet rises rapidly in the Behl household. How does one manage to strain the gravy, keep the turkey moist, and simultaneously produce the roasted (not burned) potatoes at the table? Now, *that* requires skill.

Let's talk about me again. My guests almost always marvel at my usually breezy (but composed?) mood when I am hosting a meal. One reason for this is that I am convinced there is little chance of anyone having an agreeable time if the hostess herself is not smiling, but it is primarily due to the fact that most Indian dishes can be prepared in advance and then heated just before serving—therefore, the bulk of my work is usually done beforehand. There are exceptions (such as the rice), but I often turn on the flame with the first knock at the door and my "pulau" is always perfectly ready when dinner is to be laid. (Did I just jinx these—my rice AND my mood?) The welcoming scent of basmati rice floating throughout is as enticing for your anticipatory friends as the aroma of warm, freshly baked cookies is for a potential house buyer. The real estate agent may only potentially sell the property while you will most definitely promote yourself as being the ideal host. By choosing those recipes that require the minimum of last minute attention, you will be present and able to participate in your own party too. I have clearly marked these recipes with a make-ahead note (**M/A**). Parties aside, who has the time to pull together a home-cooked meal each night of the week? Many Indian dishes keep well so you will be able to cook at one time and be prepared for an additional and bonus family dinner or two.

ACKNOWLEDGMENTS...

Thank you, Mum, for continuously nourishing me with a respect for our culture, family, friends, home, and kitchen.

Thank you, Dad, for wrapping me in an abundance of love and pride.

Thank you, Mum, Dad, and Binnie-didi.

Thank you, thank you, and thank you, Sanjay.

Thank you, Geetu, for continuously reminding me, "YES, you can!"

Thank you, India and Kargil, for choosing me—lucky, lucky me.

Thank you, Katherine, Joyce, and Christine for endlessly encouraging and elevating. I am indebted.

Thank you, Katherine, for the constant order and commitment that you have brought to my project.

Thank you, Carol...you taught me more about the power of feasting first with one's eyes (and creating desirable table habits) than you will ever know.

Thank you, Sue, for researching, photographing, and aptly capturing the essence of my table.

Thank you, Laura, for sharing your photographic expertise.

Thank you, Anna, for my flattering cover shot. You are a magician.

Thank you to my many willing friends (and friends of friends) who offered the time to test recipes and provide feedback.

Thank you to all who have attended my cooking classes—you have spurred me to no end.

Thank you, Jessica, Kelly, Ellina, Laura, Kristyn, and all at BookLogix. You managed, edited, designed, hand-held, and listened while guiding me through the process of realizing my goal.

Thank you to you for taking a look.

INTRODUCTION...

MY STORY...

It is not imperative that you read my story, but I do think that in doing so you will understand a little more about the way in which I cook and how I came to value the importance of preparing meals for myself, family, and friends. Having said that, I will never know if you skip this chapter.

I was born in Newcastle upon Tyne in the December of 1972. Newcastle is a city on the coast of northeast England. If the saying "It is like bringing coals to Newcastle" springs to mind, you are thinking of the correct place. You may also be a Newcastle Brown Ale drinker or a fan of the League Championship team, Newcastle United Football Club, which are both the main icons that promote the city to be known abroad. Newcastle also hosts the Great North Run, which is one of the world's most popular half marathons.

In earlier times, the city had grown as a center for wool trade and then as a major coal mining area. The port developed in the sixteenth century and was soon counted as one of the largest ship-building points on the global map. These industries were once exuberant but have since declined, and today, Newcastle is largely a business, educational, and cultural center, with a reputation for a buzzing nightlife.

In 1955 my father immigrated to England. The opportunity to "have a better life" and partake in a growing economy was the draw. He recounts leaving Bandala, a village in The Punjab (a northwestern state of India), boarding *The Victory* (a Polish ship) in Mumbai, and docking at the Port of Southampton (on the coast of southern England) on November 7. My dad remembers being offered a chocolate bar on his two-week, rocky voyage (a "Kit Kat" to be precise). "Cadbury" being one of the few English words my dad could read at the time, he grabbed it, inhaled it, and went on to "womit wiolently" (that is, "throw up"

to you and me). That twelve-year-old boy has never willingly touched a piece of chocolate again.

My father, his siblings, and my grandmother traveled north to Newcastle where my grandfather (who had already arrived five years earlier—soon after the partition of British India in 1947) had been able to secure a job and rent a home. The children enrolled at the local school and when finished found work... the aim being to earn and save enough money to open one's own business. My dad's first place of employment was at the shipyards, and even today, he so fondly speaks of tiring but jovial times. As one Punjabi family relocated to Newcastle, other family members and friends followed. Soon there was a small but vibrant Hindu Punjabi community flourishing and establishing itself. (Today the population in Greater Newcastle is just under 300,000. People of Indian descent comprise approximately 1.5 percent of this number.) All dreamed the same hopes of inventing a comfortable life for themselves and their children in this foreign land while trying to integrate yet uphold their own culture and beliefs.

When my dad was twenty-five years old, he and six of his Indian friends left for India within weeks of one another in order to each find a bride. One by one, again within weeks of one another, they returned with bulging suitcases, sticky sweets, gifts, amusing stories, pride, and oh...their wives. Ever seen the movie *Seven Brides for Seven Brothers*? These seven "arrangements" materialized almost as quickly as those on the cinema screen.

Now is where I manage to get a little more detail. My mum left New Delhi and recalls landing at London Heathrow Airport on July 14, 1969. The following morning she pulled into Newcastle Central Train Station, and she paints a picture of the cold, damp weather that she had never before experienced. This was her first taste of her new home—her roll of the dice. My dad told her that it was only going to get colder as July was actually one of the warmer months in England. This reality was only the initial surprise. Although my mother was more than (coyly) ecstatic with her parents' choice of husband for her (if you are ever fortunate enough to meet my dad, you will surely realize that he truly is an amazing being, truly), she now laughs at the changes that fate had brought her way. She and the other wives had to learn to live a hugely different life from their time in India. Most daughters from comfortable homes in India were not required to cook, clean, work, or drive. Overnight, my mum was pretty much doing it all.

So, my mum learned to cook for her husband, her in-laws, and all the new friends that visited too. She did not do it alone. This was a communal act of the mother-in-law, the daughters-in-law, and the sisters-in-law laying out dinner as a family. She speedily became a triumphant cook (even if after a few hiccups and private lessons—my dad would furtively teach my mum how to knead the dough and roll "chapattis" while she would guard the kitchen door for fear of being found out). It may always have been within her to showcase these unknown skills, or it may have accidentally occurred due to a yearning to recreate the tastes that she was missing from back home. My mum could not imagine eating the mussels, oysters, and other fried crustaceans that my father had appreciatively learned to savor on the docks. She detested the idea of traditional Christmas lunch without lashings of Tabasco sauce (this still happens today), and she was frustrated by the lack of high-quality spices available in the one Indian grocery store in Newcastle at that time. She was, however, elated to receive the crates of Deshari and Alphonso

mangoes that my grandparents in New Delhi would send—a sure tonic to buoy homesick spirits. My paternal grandmother would summon the extended family over in order to divide these precious fruits. My grandmother would argue that a home that does not distribute its good fortune will never prosper. This is a lesson my mum modeled for me, and it is one that I have tried to adhere to. When reappearing from visits to India, my mum would be laden with and exhibit pickles, spices, and roasted nuts that would once again attract many local visitors. The need to pay the savvy businessman who would drive 300 miles down to London to shop for (and hence sell) these ethnic groceries was thankfully put aside for a month or two.

The number of Punjabi families continued to grow, and the demand for Indian food stores, vinyl-record shops, sari fabric boutiques, and a Hindu Temple all emerged.

My mum began to assimilate in the city she now called home. When she could not find an ingredient, she and my many "aunties" (who had also witnessed the same personal turn of events) would search for and substitute a close second. One such example is the dense "stotty cake" (a bread originating in the northeast of England) in place of the Punjabi "kulcha" bread that is a perfect pairing with spiced chickpeas. I, of course, did not miss the original kulcha but understood something of the void while viewing the film version of the acclaimed novel *The Namesake* (by Jhumpa Lahiri). The bride arrives from India in the USA in the 1970s and uses rice krispie cereal as a substitute for "bhel" (a puffed rice used to make a popular savory Mumbai street food). Just so you know, bhel is found in most Indian food stores abroad today. An aside—it is now I who fondly remembers the stotty cake.

April 19, 1969..."I do..."

The honeymoon begins...

At the Taj Mahal, India.

Exploring Newcastle, England.

The irony is that before long and due to a rising demand (late 1970s and early 1980s), the Indian ingredients that were exported and becoming available in cities such as Newcastle were of a superior quality to those bought in the local stores in India. My mum's words—not mine. Oh and here is a twist—she started packing cheddar cheese, strawberry jam, and whole-nut chocolates on her travels in order to spread her discoveries with our family back home.

Just to make you smile—one of my aunties has never even feigned an interest in entering the kitchen, so she recounts her early days in the UK as being less about searching for missing ingredients and more to do with secretly admiring the novelty of blond, blue-eyed, fair-skinned Englishmen who happened to cross her fortunate path (usually in Woolworth's). My sentiments were not too dissimilar when first arriving in Georgia. Yes, I had known fair-skinned Englishmen, but I had never before been—Rhett-Butler-style—poetically addressed by one as "ma'am." Southern drawl and imaginary movie sets became my everyday.

Back to Newcastle...by the time my sister and I arrived on the scene, my parents were running their own retail clothing business. Financially speaking, matters were booming. Was this because of their committed efforts or because the Chopra family had been blessed with two daughters (versions of "Laxmi," the goddess of wealth)? Many would say the former; my parents always believed the latter. It is still a belief in many Hindu homes that Laxmis are a bonus but that little "Kings" are a *must*. I am thankful that my sister and I were born as and remained as "musts."

My mother worked part-time alongside my father in their business and was usually the one to collect us from school. We always came home to our first dinner of the evening...yes, you read it correctly. We would eat at four and then again at eight when my dad got home. Apart from my Punjabi genes, I confidently blame my inability to ever fit into skinny jeans as having something to do with the above! We will let bygones be bygones, but neither my head nor my tummy ever did comprehend why my non-Indian friends would offer me a clementine during an afternoon playdate, but my sister was at home, chowing down a bountiful helping of "biryani" (a flavorful meat and rice dish) at the exact same hour. An act of love? Mmm...

Although my parents no longer lived in the same house as my grandparents, our lives were still very much entwined. We ate dinner at my grandmother's home with my aunties, uncles, and cousins every Saturday evening. Even if it was a short night, it was expected, and we all looked forward to it. As was so often stated, if we ate together, we would stay together. In addition, it would be at least twice a week when bidding goodnight to the grown-ups in our sitting room would be a production in itself because there happened to be so many of them. They would primarily consist of my grandmother, her sister, her sisters-in-law, her niece, and any adult daughters or sisters that happened to be around. I stress the female members of the group because it is they that I spent most time with—the men often sat in another room. Culturally, this was prevalent at the time. The children were to be seen, and when addressed, the response was expected to be spoken in (conversational) Punjabi or Hindi—not the scripted, dramatic dialogue characteristic of

Hindi cinema that we were encouraged to watch. I am reminded of the night that my cousin implored our granddad to stand up for him (much as grandparents are often requested to do against their own children). My cousin dared our "Baa-ji" to show due hero-like courage if, as a child, he had been nursed upon his own mother's breast milk. "Jai ho!" More forceful prayers and regular visits to the Temple ensued. In addition to the VHS and family time, the evening was really about the food (much of it) being served. It did not matter if they started at eight, nine, or ten o'clock, the same amount of eating went on. My mum would offer something repeatedly until it was taken (the behavior of a polite hostess). The guest would refuse enough times so as not to appear greedy but then gladly receive it (the actions of a polite visitor).

The plates were perpetually wiped clean yet the giving of comments regarding the improvement or success of the dish was never shied from. My mother had grown to be a superb cook—quite the heroine (as I said earlier, as a result of desperation or opportunity, we will never know)—and I only recall hearing compliment after compliment about her creations. The kitchen continuously smelled inviting, a ludicrous amount of "ghee" (clarified butter) was often being prepared, raw nuts were being roasted with cumin and chili powder (even today, these descriptions tease my senses and evoke comforting moods and images), and the young Chopra girls were being told to watch and learn. Each time my mother called upon me to chop, knead, observe, and absorb a step in the process of some concoction and I refused (a universal mother/daughter issue?), I was stared in the eye and firmly posed with the rhetorical question of "What will your mother-in-law say?" I never really understood the meaning behind my mother's demand until much later but knew enough that it was important to roll up my sleeves and attack the task I had been assigned. When a girl from the Punjabi, Hindu community marries, it is said that she is reborn into her second and permanent home. Her successful assimilation into the new home and her behavior as a daughter-in-law, sister-in-law, wife, and future mother is a reflection of the household from which she has come. It follows then, that if at any time in the future I could not put a substantial and delicious meal on the table, my mother would scandalously be up for blame—she was covering her own back! I am taking liberties now but do not want to in any way undermine my parents' beliefs—I profoundly respect their faith and teaching. I did watch and I did learn—I did this because I was expected to but also because I wanted to. (Incidentally, "What does my mother-in-law say?" Well, it is with surety, I can confide that she has never had cause to complain).

So, for as far back as I can remember, my own mum has stressed the gravity of laying out a memorable meal and maintains that to bring joy to a husband is to feed him well (...years later, I have still not told her that I think I found another way).

I regularly attempted something new in the kitchen and was continually signing up for cooking classes, whether they were Chinese, Italian, or Moroccan. My friends visited and benefited from the results of my fervent dabbling. Because of this penchant for cooking and a spirit for teaching, I was forever found pottering "gourmand fashion" in the kitchen, addressing an imaginary and attentive audience while describing the method of putting together whatever it was that was evolving at my hands. I reveled in watching Madhur Jaffrey, Delia Smith, and later Nigella Lawson delight in uncovering their culinary secrets and tips on the telly. (Nowadays, I can sit for hours fascinated before and under the supreme influence of Gordon Ramsay, Giada, Barefoot Contessa, Jamie Oliver, and yes, always...Nigella—her oh so typical and natural command of throwing sultry kitchen glances is my chief culinary goal.)

In 1995 I graduated from The University of Northumbria with a Bachelor's degree in Early Education. I spent two years teaching in a nearby village school. They were two of the most contented years of my life. I adored being "Miss Chopra," I cherished the curiosity-filled children I was so fortunate to educate, and I appreciated the immensely supportive, trusting parents and the team of seasoned teachers who guided me. Then, one Thursday evening, I came upon my mum, all in a tizzy—slicing, frying, and juggling more than was necessary for a weeknight dinner. Fluttery and frantic and anxious and loquacious and ridiculously upbeat—visualize someone akin to Mrs. Bennett's character from the classic novel *Pride and Prejudice*—that was my mum. Appalled at my lack of desire to help contain this escalating chaos, she proudly proclaimed that a "very nice, suitable, Indian boy" from America was coming to meet me. The motive was clear—unsaid but understood. The introduction, like others before, did not concern me; it was the "from America" that did. I objected, only to hear that he was already on a flight to London and would be at our dining table by five on Friday afternoon. His first dinner with us had to be beyond comparison. Hearty, homey food would inevitably lure this suitor—whom, incidentally, my parents had not yet met—right into proposing to me. Rumor had it that our horoscopes were a blazing astrological match.

Needless to say, they allowed him to assume that I had solely devised and cooked the entire feast. My parents fell in love with my husband immediately. Just so you know, he never did propose to me—still a sore point. Soon after, we were engaged, the date was set, and our relatives and friends from India, all over the UK, and beyond arrived to celebrate this weeklong fiesta. Sanjay (my go-to regarding "real" India) says that the Punjabi customs so strongly upheld in Newcastle at that time were similar to those of The Punjab in the fifties—an "anthropologist's delight." Personifying a thread, woven amongst the details of this cross-generational and culturally rich tapestry, warms my thankful soul. The wedding was certainly a party and depicted scenes (and beings) that can be likened to those from the movies *Bend It Like Beckham* and *My Big Fat Greek Wedding*—a lot of jewelry, a lot of Scotch, and a lot more cleavage than was necessary. If only I had known how to jiggle like those sparkly-sari-clad Bollywood starlets, the ability to manage a kitchen might not have even entered the equation. My husband was wise, focused, and ready to be a doting partner. I was not sure if I could be the wife that an Indian man, from India, would want. He told me that it was I who was the conservative half of the marriage, having chosen to marry a traditional man from "the village." That, he was not. He was, in fact, well traveled, well educated, beyond handsome, and wanting to build a home and family. I wanted the same. Sometimes our parents (or is it our gods and goddesses?) just know. This really has nothing to do with food and is a separate story entirely but one that most people we meet are keen to hear a little about. No, we did not know one another. I will leave it once I tell you that his first shock became apparent on our wedding night, having discovered that this British-Indian did not floss. Thank goodness I had the ring and he had accepted the goat, two camels, and an elephant, or else this might have been a deal-breaker! He hastily took responsibility for his bride's flaw, fixed it on the very same night, and I shortly after flaunted gleaming teeth and began to feel for him the way my whole family already did.

Two days later we were in Fontainebleau, France. Sanjay was pursuing an MBA program, and we would be living in this fairytale town for close to a year. Okay, a food lover in France? I was eating Brie and grapes for breakfast by day three. By day five, champagne was included with most evening meals, and before I knew it, I had had my first taste of foie gras, escargots, and an authentic quiche Lorraine. Myself and the other wives, girlfriends, and partners who had made the *sacrifice* to move to this university town from our respective countries were not pining too loudly for home. We took complete advantage of the situation and ate together, drank together, explored the capital together, and took French cooking classes while our spouses hit the books day after day. I learned so much about world cultures, traditions, customs, and food during this time. I am certain that my friends feel the same. My year-long honeymoon was a lesson in understanding that my way is not the only way, and I will forever remember my days there. A friend showed me how to make cannelloni, another how to prepare moussaka, and yet another how to perfect the art of setting the table. Between exam week and study groups, Sanjay and I ventured to vineyards in Bordeaux and made short trips to Andorra, Barcelona, Amsterdam, Cyprus, and Prague. What I mean to say is that I know that the way in which I host a party, finalize a menu, create a dish, and greet my guests is all a glorious culmination of the obvious Indian element in my upbringing and my life in Newcastle and in France—a kaleidoscope of my being. I confidently adopt the notion that "fusion" does not always equal "confusion." On the contrary, food stylist Aran Goyagoa speaks mountains to me—she believes that while cooking, knowing and representing yourself allows the finished meal to reflect you and therefore make complete sense to those you have included at your table. It follows then that your table is, in fact, an extension of your being.

By the end of 1998, we were residing in London. I was teaching in a respectable preparatory school, and my husband had secured a position with a leading consulting firm. It was a fabulous two years. I could visit "home, home" (Newcastle) regularly and connect and eat with my parents at their table. Back in London, we sampled amazing Indian food in some renowned restaurants and in some holes in the wall. I started making more and more of my mum's dishes at home. The ground was not as treacherous as I had imagined. It was the opposite—it was exhilarating when I realized that I was somewhat competently able to reinvent these tastes, and it spurred me to experiment with more, seemingly taxing recipes.

My husband's job then relocated us to Atlanta, Georgia. My flight from Heathrow via Paris landed on July 7, 2000. Sanjay had already arrived to pave the way. The bus that drives one from the flight's exit to the terminal building did not appear, so myself and my fellow passengers disembarked and scurried through a blanket of suffocating humidity to the airport entrance. I thought my travels had transported me to New Delhi! Sanjay tells me that his plan was that I would first experience Atlanta at its hottest—it would only get better. It did become cooler and did get better...much better. I enrolled in graduate school to

study for a Master's degree in Education ("Radhika" was difficult for many of my peers to pronounce so I somehow morphed into "Erotica"—that is another conversation entirely). We bought a home, we made lifelong friends, we were blessed with our children, and my life, as I now know it, began.

Do I miss the UK? Without a doubt—I do not see my family and friends enough, I surprisingly still miss the colder weather, I miss warming my tights on the radiator, I miss the ease of walking to places and using the London Underground, and occasionally I long for "fish fingers" or a "cheese pasty." I soon learned that I also yearn for the aunties who have no qualms about extending their judgment, histories, and advice and yet willingly lend their ears and open their kitchens and hearts to me. This has not changed, it is just that now I am only steeped in it once a year.

My children will never regularly experience these crazy but oh-so-cherished happenings.

Is Atlanta home? Without a doubt. Leaving England, many people asked me if I had seen the movie *Gone with the Wind* and warned that Atlanta may not welcome an Indian from England. They were wrong. This city has rendered us an extended family, a rewarding place to work...and drive-throughs! We have experienced nothing but southern hospitality. As part and parcel of the many renowned restaurants that Atlanta has birthed, we have particularly appreciated the typical fried green tomatoes and chicken, collard greens, slow roasted pork ribs, and outrageous macaroni and cheese. Sweetened iced tea is something I neither care for nor will ever understand. My world cracked open and has continued to grow. I now know who Rosa Parks is, I comprehend why the entire country halts for the Super Bowl, and I am eternally grateful to be

surrounded by those I care for at Thanksgiving. Life has me smiling, and I am thankful for it all—a pool (and pool boy) would only frame the picture.

My children were born here, and their arrival helped me lay a foundation for my adopted home. I have wholeheartedly hurled myself into seeing this as our life. Atlanta will always be "home, home" for my babies...at least I hope that they will sense the belonging that accompanies being able to call something one's own. This is evident when we Behls are amongst the first to lay down our picnic blankets in anticipation of the July 4 celebrations. "Own" for them should absolutely signify those Independence Day fireworks yet also include their Indian legacy. When immediate relatives are not close by and trips home are fewer than liked, then food is often the way to ensure this bond. It is through our mealtimes that I hope pleasurable memories will emerge and thus cement the tie for India and Kargil. I am a firm believer in what is meant to be will be, yet I am still extremely mindful of the role I want to play in what that may be. I intentionally use our table to feed the relationship between parent and child, brother and sister, and home and heritage.

We try to eat an Indian dinner four or five nights per week. My insistence on this is not because the meal has to be Indian to be healthy but because in providing this, my children are sure to eat the same foods that Grandma and Granddad lay out when we visit both India and the UK. A catalyst for bonding? A secure and common arena in which to spend family mealtimes? A lesson in our own cultural identity and traditions? An opportunity to embrace and celebrate our own? As I have defined, for me it is all of the above.

It is truly an added bonus for my family when I read of the medicinal benefits of many commonly used ingredients. Today, this news is at the forefront of healthy eating. Now my persistence has become an acceptable part of our life at the table. Is it not too spicy for the children? Remember, you can lessen the amount of chili powder or any other flavor or spice that you add. I will remind you as you read on. Furthermore, we always serve plain yogurt as a condiment, and generally speaking, children add a little extra of this "coolant" to where the hot spice lies. The composition of an Indian meal easily lends itself to include vegetables and grains. If buying organic—meats (vegetarian-fed and humanely raised) and

dairy too—the level of benefits is once again increased. If the cook is able to include whole grain rice, then, with all in tandem, it is a home run. These are all small steps that I, too, am teaching myself to make as I write and research the facts. I am not a nutritionist but am satisfied knowing that I am doing some things right—not only for my children but for myself too. The kitchen is the core of our home. My intent is not to feed but to "nourish" and continue to "replenish" our unit. Contemplate...nutritional, well-balanced, gratifying, and painless-to-prepare Indian dishes? I am about to show you how.

WHAT IS NORTH INDIAN FOOD?

The recipes I have included are from North India and more specifically from the State of Punjab. These are the dishes that I have grown up on. As I have mentioned, I am not a professional chef nor do I profess to be a Madhur Jaffrey, Tarla Dalal, or Padma Lakshmi (although I will, one day, have legs like hers—perhaps in this lifetime...but more probably in my next), but I will promise you that these recipes will work. Some may question the authenticity of the recipes as I have made the preparation of some plates simpler than is usual. Some may ask if my ideas are a fusion of thoughts. Yes, a patchwork of experiences has shaped what I am presenting to you. Think of me as being a bridge that beckons a more modern approach to the conventional home cooking of my mum's Punjabi kitchen.

Traditionally, this style of cuisine includes both non-vegetarian and completely vegetarian dishes as many Indians are born into a vegetarian or vegan lifestyle.

The food can typically be described as rich, as it calls for the inclusion of butter and cream. This was customary years ago because most of the rural landowners and workforce in The Punjab required enough fuel to keep them operational in the fields. Popular "paneer" dishes, "pakoras," "samosas," and "naan" bread are the more well-known elements of Punjabi cuisine.

It may soon come to your attention that there is no beef included in any of my dishes. My religion is Hinduism, and its social customs do not permit the consumption of beef. The cow is considered "mother-like" as it is a provider of milk, and hence the eating of the animal was banned. My son once accidentally ate a hamburger. Finding out, I explained the illogical difference between "ham" and "hamburger" and that it was an acceptable mistake. With brimming tears, his closing comment before bed was, "I will never, ever do it again...but it was really good." (I have also heard countless tales of Indian vegetarians who have newly arrived in the US or the UK and have unknowingly bitten into and satiatingly wolfed down a "cheese" burger. Holy cow!)

Pork is also omitted from the book. The pig is thought of as being unclean in most Hindu homes—it is not banned, however. For me, an overloaded bacon and egg sandwich can be described as messy but *never* unclean! The point is that I have not included these meats in the recipes I am presenting, but if you are inclined, try substituting and see what comes your way. You will observe that with practice you will gain the confidence to add a little more or less of something as your tastes and understanding develop.

I once heard a TV chef (I wish I could remember who) capture his audience (namely me) with the following temptation, "I am giving you a step-by-step invitation to cook—no strings attached. You'll find yourself becoming excited...I urge you to take the risk and consider abandoning all precautions." I am not sure why exactly, but I blushed, laughed, and took his advice—dinner and dessert were mind-blowing that night. Now, I am inviting you...

SPICES AND HERBS (AND OTHER BASIC INGREDIENTS) IN THE PUNJABI KITCHEN...

A **spice** is a dried seed, fruit, root, or bark (of vegetable origin) that is used for the purpose of adding flavor, color, scent, and/or as a preservative whilst cooking. I have learned that many spices are used for medicinal purposes too.

An **herb** is taken from the leafy green part of a plant. It may be fresh or dried and is included in a dish for flavor, color, or scent. I have also learned that many use herbs for medicinal purposes too.

You will notice that I have specified a time for the spice or (dried) herb to cook in most of my recipes. This allows a release of flavors and aromas and eliminates the risk of any unpleasant or sand-like aftertaste. Although freshly grinding can also add a deep dimension to your dish, I have to be honest when I say that I really only (sometimes) take the time for black pepper—the rest, I buy. I have had no complaints yet. Speaking of buying, I suggest that you visit your local Indian/Eastern ethnic store or farmers' market. The spices are likely to be fresh (as the turnover is regular), and the prices will probably beat any regular grocery store. Online is also a super option nowadays. How easy is that?

If you switch on the news or open a magazine these days, you are bound to hear something with regard to recent health research and the positive effects of some commonly used ingredients. It is almost comical to my mum that these are touted as "new" discoveries. As many proud cultures exclaim, "*We* have been doing this for years," and the Indian race is no exception to claiming authority in understanding this domain.

I will outline what I have learned about the medicinal and health properties of certain ingredients that I use in my home. I do this in no particular order. There are many more ingredients that may be used in Indian cuisine, but I have described only those that I include in my own preparations. Do not be daunted by this information—at the very least, these properties can only bring an added level of knowledge and nourishment to your home, and I confidently vouch that I do use some of these spices and herbs more regularly if a particular remedy is called for. I am almost always amazed at the results. I do not know the science but all that I have learned has been extracted from my family, news shows, the Internet, and an array of magazines and well-being books. I am merely offering you food for thought—there is a wealth of literature to browse if you are so inclined.

As I wrap up my introduction to the next few pages, please note that when one chooses to cook an Indian meal, one must attempt to embrace the philosophy of the Indian kitchen—that is, that there are no hard and fast stipulations. If there is one, be sure that I will make it clear to you. If you just cannot abide the flavor of cilantro, do not garnish your finished plate with it. If you relish the spiciness of fresh ginger but your stomach is wary of red chili, simply add more and less respectively. It will become apparent that few of my recipes include garlic, and this is because my dad has an extreme aversion to the scent. It was never included as an ingredient and my taste buds were "de-garlicized" forever. It is, however,

a common ingredient in most Punjabi homes, so please do not hesitate to peel, smash, chop, and add alongside the onion at your own will.

Store spices and dry herbs in airtight boxes and in a dark cupboard. Take care to scoop them out using a dry spoon, as any moisture will probably lessen the shelf life of the seasoning. If you notice a slight discoloration as time goes on, do not fret—while the appearance may have changed, the flavor will not have altered significantly.

"garam masala" literally means "hot spices" and is a combination of cinnamon, cloves, cumin, black pepper, and occasionally bay leaves and fennel seeds depending upon the "secret" family recipe. My mum makes her own (I am gifted much of it), but (much to her exasperation) I am also more than content to buy it ready-mixed and ground. Some blend and freshly grind the ingredients in the required quantity just before using—my question is "why?" There are numerous varieties out there. It brings an abundance of flavor and aroma and is included in the base of most of my recipes. A must-have in the Indian kitchen. Which one should you buy? If I am spoilt for choice, I choose the darker/richer colored blend.

turmeric ("haldi") is most commonly used in its powdered form. It is thought to possess anti-inflammatory properties, lessen the risk of gallstones and stomach issues, and aid with the control of diabetes. It is currently being investigated widely as regards its possible positive effect upon cancer, arthritis, and Alzheimer's disease. Be careful—it stains. The face, arms, and legs of the Hindu bride- and groom-to-be are smeared with a smooth turmeric paste before they bathe, in order to ensure a healthy glow (for the big day) and to promote fertility (for *after* the big day!)

red chili powder ("lal mirch") purely consists of ground, red chilis and no other spices. You will sometimes see "extra hot" chili powder in the Indian spice section, which is also perfectly fine to buy, but use it sparingly as it may be fiery. The strength of heat in a chili powder depends upon the original chilis used and their capsaicin content in particular. Apparently helps lower cholesterol and speed up metabolism—yes, another bowl of hot and sour soup please!

cumin seeds ("jeera") can be ground, but I really only ever use them whole (except for the occasional recipe where the seed may change the overall texture of the dish). They are considered to be an aid to digestion and bloating (steep 1/2 teaspoon in a cup of boiling water for some relief, ladies). Cumin is a source of iron and manganese and is also said to strengthen the immune system.

black pepper ("kali mirch") is always at its best when freshly ground, but then I am not always at my best so I do not fret over reaching into a packet. This spice relieves indigestion and bloating and has anti-bacterial and antioxidant properties, so why not just add a pinch to almost anything savory that you are preparing? When I have a cold or a cough, I take a 1/2 teaspoon of black pepper and a little freshly grated ginger, and I boil it with water, tea, and milk. I drink it hot to help clear my sinuses—my voice (to my husband's dismay) is back in no time.

pomegranate powder ("anardana") is the dried, ground seeds of the pomegranate fruit. This spice adds a distinct tartness to any dish, and its flavor is popular in Middle Eastern cuisines as well as Indian. It is simply exquisite when used in the marinade for lamb or added to garbanzo beans/chickpeas. High in antioxidants, it is said to help insomniacs sleep better, reduce blood pressure, increase blood flow, be beneficial to the functioning of the heart, and is also being regarded as a preventative for prostate and skin cancers. If you cannot locate it, substitute with mango powder.

mango powder ("amchur/amchoor") is the result of drying and grinding the flesh and rind of an unripe mango. No one I know has attempted this—save everyone the trouble and just buy it. The powder has a noticeable taste—tart and acidic and pairs well with meat, poultry, and fish. You will see that I use it with potatoes and eggplant as a souring agent too. It contains iron and vitamins A and E, but I doubt that you will get huge benefits from it with the small amount that one would realistically consume—just good to know.

dry fenugreek leaves ("sukhi/kasoori/quasuri methi") have a distinct and robust taste and aroma—remember, a little goes a long way. The fresh leaf is prepared something like spinach, but it is not really available in the regular grocery store. The dried herb is a great addition to many meat, vegetable, and bread dishes. Some suggest sprinkling over as a garnish before serving, but I prefer to add during the cooking process for a release of flavors. It is believed to increase the flow of breast milk and to lower cholesterol levels.

red chili flakes/crushed red chili are dried and crushed red chili peppers. They usually have a smoky flavor. I use when I want the seed to be apparent in the dish—especially in chutneys and in my chocolate/chili sauce. Flakes or powder—the choice is yours.

carom seeds ("ajwain") is sometimes referred to as "bishops' weed." It is a great tonic for stomach or intestinal discomfort. While nursing my daughter, India, my mum would encourage me to drink water that she had infused overnight with the herb. It is firmly believed to reduce the baby's gassiness. It was either the ajwain or the tummy rubs that did the trick.

cinnamon ("dalchini") speeds up your metabolism. Who knew? It has a strong but pleasant flavor and aroma and is considered to offer a multitude of health benefits in the Indian kitchen. It is an effective remedy for the common cold, it stimulates digestion, checks nausea, and is said to support the natural production of insulin. That cinnamon-roll bun was not such a mistake after all! Make a cinnamon chai (tea) and reap the rewards.

green cardamom seeds ("elaichi dana") helps to aid digestion, stomach problems, and heartburn. Chewing on this sweet aromatic spice serves as a breath freshener for many in India.

green cardamom pods ("choti elaichi") actually hold the cardamom seeds. Just open up and include only the seeds or throw in the cracked-open pod too and allow the flavor to impart. Discard the green skin when the dish is complete.

cloves ("laung") will work miracles with a toothache and sore gums—although quite pungent, you might place one against the painful area, and you will feel some relief. It is also believed to help ease arthritic pain. Grind the cloves or remove from the dish before serving, as finding yourself chewing on a whole one is not often a pleasing experience. Used in sweet and savory preparations.

black cardamom pods ("moti elaichi") are used widely in Chinese medicine as a "wisdom enhancer" as they are thought to promote intelligence. Eases digestion, constipation, and urinary tract problems. Included in sweet and savory dishes but most often consumed when added to milk-based desserts or tea. Crack open to gain the maximum flavor.

dry bay leaves ("tej patta") have a slightly floral scent. I use the dry leaf because they are so readily available. Remove from the pan after cooking as they are very chewy and may leave a nasty aftertaste if you accidentally come upon one. Apparently, boiling fresh bay leaves in water and adding that infused water to your bath will ease muscle and joint pain...I say give it a shot but take a vodka/lime/soda along with you too!

ginger powder ("saunth") I drank ginger tea by the bucket-load during both of my pregnancies. It really does prevent nausea, and it has a calming effect as well as having the reputation of curing colds, coughs, and migraines...there is a reason your grandma gave you ginger ale when your tummy was doing somersaults. Fresh ginger is used in most of my dishes as it has a different flavor to the ground version, so opt for the root if you are able. Ginger powder is a substitute in an emergency but perfectly acceptable in tea or baked goods. I tested that about 1/8 teaspoon is close to the equivalent of 1 teaspoon of freshly grated ginger.

fennel seeds/aniseed ("saunf") supposedly strengthens eyesight, increases the flow of breast milk, and is an effective diuretic when chewed regularly. It is sometimes taken after the meal as it has an inviting, floral, "anise-like" aroma. You will probably spot a bowl of it at the exit of your local Indian restaurant—I prefer a sealed packet as opposed to the communal dish, thank you very much!

saffron ("kesar") is most largely produced in Spain and then in India. It is one of the most expensive spices as the labor involved in harvesting it is tremendous. The threads add a richness, depth, and sunny tinge of yellow to the fellow ingredients. Soak a small amount in warm water or milk before adding to the dish in order to release the color. Although the flavor is subtle, it will bring your plate alive—but do not overdo it. It has been reported to alleviate depression, asthma, and fatigue.

black mustard seeds ("rai") are often included in pickles, chutneys, and salads. The popular Dijon mustard is made from this variety of mustard seed.

split moong beans/lentils ("dhooli moong/mung dal"—washed)
are produced by removing the outer layer of the whole mung bean and splitting the kernel
(see below).

whole mung beans ("moong/mung dal"—whole) are used as pictured, but just
so you know, splitting this bean yields the split moong/mung bean lentil (see above).

Bengal gram dal ("chana dal") is produced by removing the outer layer of the "black
garbanzo bean/chickpea" and splitting the kernel.

kidney beans ("rajma")

black-eyed peas ("rongi," "lobia," or "chawli")

black/mapte lentils ("urad dal"—whole)

garbanzo beans/chickpeas ("chana")—I only use the dried variety of any bean, lentil, or pulse, but I do use canned garbanzo beans regularly as they hold their form and absorb flavors well.

curry powder—I feel the need to explain that the North Indian home cook does not utilize curry powder (at least for his/her Indian preparations). It is actually a blend of spices—a Western invention. The word "curry" is thought to be a British corruption of the word "kadi" which means something akin to "with sauce." There are regional versions of "kadi" all over India—each version varies and is typical of the cuisine in question. However, I do not doubt it to be a "must-have" ingredient for a traditionally English, curried "Coronation Chicken."

FRESH PRODUCE SECTION OF GROCERY STORE:

fresh cilantro/coriander—rinse the whole bunch, wrap in a paper towel to dry, chop using a knife and board or kitchen scissors. A common garnish for the finished dish. It is rarely used to garnish green vegetables. I am certain that my mum would deem her dinner to be ruined if she found she had forgotten to buy this most essential herb.

fresh mint—remove the leaves from their stems, rinse, wrap in a paper towel to dry, chop using a knife and board or kitchen scissors.

onions—I always use white or yellow onions unless specified. However, if I only have a red one left in my basket, it will not stop me from preparing dinner.

fresh ginger—take the root, peel or scrape off the skin. Grate as you wish—finely or coarsely. My mum regularly buys a crate of fresh ginger and then settles to spend a late night before her Indian soap operas—she painstakingly peels and chops. The result being a swollen Ziploc bag or two for the freezer. She simply reaches in and breaks off the desired portion when and as she needs it.

tomatoes—a fundamental ingredient in many of the dishes that you will learn to cook. Fresh is naturally the best option, but I do keep the cartons or cans of chopped/crushed tomatoes on hand—an ideal go-to for Indian cuisine.

tomato paste/puree—you will find this in a can or tube. It consists of concentrated tomatoes (the skin and seeds are removed) and results from the reduction of the fruit to a thick paste.

fresh garlic—tease the clove from bulb. Firmly smash with the back of a knife. Remove the peel. Chop on a board. Rub your hands with lemon juice to minimize the odor. (I do not use garlic very much.)

serrano chilis—take off the top. Lie the chili flat on a chopping board and slice lengthways. Remove the membranes and seeds if they scare you (this will reduce the heat). Chop. Wash hands!

jalapeno peppers—as above. Jalapeno peppers have less capsaicin (heat) than the serrano chili so judge your own threshold.

potatoes—I use white or yellow potatoes. Yukon gold or Idaho appear in my vegetable basket most often. However, I am not particularly fussy.

lemons—the juice and rind offers an acidity that is characteristic of many Indian dishes. Note: a lemon at room-temperature will yield the most juice.

REFRIGERATED SECTION OF GROCERY STORE:

butter—I will specify whether it should be salted or not.

plain yogurt—I usually buy the low- or reduced-fat (rarely the fat-free) kind to eat alongside a dish or when preparing "raita" (see "Accompaniments" section). I choose Greek or whole-milk yogurt when making the dish just a tad more special. We often eat the yogurt plain and as a "cooling" condiment alongside the rest of the meal.

"paneer"—this is an unaged, acid-set, non-melting farmer cheese (or curd cheese). It is made by curdling heated milk with the assistance of lemon juice or vinegar. My mum uses white vinegar. Rennet is not used as the coagulation agent, so this makes the paneer completely vegetarian and provides one of the main sources of protein for strict vegetarians in India. You will find it in your local Indian grocery store or farmers' market—most often in the freezer section. It may be in a frozen, block form (which is easy enough to cube or crumble once defrosted) or previously cubed and then frozen or cubed, fried, and then packaged and frozen. Some places will offer fresh paneer, and such stores are a great resource for many Indians who no longer have the desire to make their own at home. I think I have made my own cheese thrice...well...maybe twice. I am not sharing a recipe (because I do not have one), so I suggest that you buy it in the Indian store or farmers' market—just as I do.

STAPLES SECTION OF GROCERY STORE:

oil—I use canola oil in my Indian recipes, but any flavorless vegetable oil would be perfect too. No olive oil—its flavor contests with the spices.

rice—I only use "basmati" rice because that is what my mum uses. It has a unique fragrance and long-grain and most of its production is in The Punjab region of India. Available in both white and brown varieties. I'm learning to include the latter. Buy it in your local grocery store, the Indian store, or the farmers' market. (Wash rice well before use.)

atta flour—a whole-wheat flour made from hard wheat grown across the Indian sub-continent. Used for most Indian breads. Buy it in the Indian store or farmers' market.

gram flour ("besan")—this is made from ground garbanzo beans/chickpeas. Gluten-free, FYI. Buy it in the Indian store or the farmers' market.

semolina flour ("suji"/"sooji")—the gritty, coarse particles of wheat left after the finer flour has been sifted. Buy it in your local grocery store, the Indian store, or the farmers' market.

nuts—almonds, cashews, and pistachios are frequently used in my kitchen. Always use the unsalted kind unless specified. I store in the fridge until I need them.

sugar—I use brown sugar but white sugar will work just as well.

A NOTE OR TWO BEFORE WE START...

Here are a few pointers that may guide you as you explore my recipes and the Indian kitchen. If I am sharing what you already know, forgive me and just move on:

Serves: The number of servings that I offer is only an estimation—you understand better than anyone if your friends and family peck like birds or boast voracious appetites. Judge accordingly.

Preparation time: I give an accurate estimate. Please accept a slight variation as being the result of the chef's mood.

Cooking time: I give an accurate estimate. Please accept a slight variation as being the result of the obvious differences between the temperature controls in my own and your kitchen.

Notes: I will offer a note or tip if I feel that I have a worthy one.

Serving suggestion: I am often asked which dishes work well together or to order when going to an Indian restaurant. Even more queries arise while planning such a menu at home. I have proposed some possibilities. It may be the way I have always eaten the dish or the way in which I have seen it presented elsewhere. I hasten to add that these ideas are merely suggestions. There are no rules. Enjoy as you wish.

M/A: I will tell you whether or not the recipe may be made ahead.

* I will tell you whether or not the dish freezes well.

Measurements:

tablespoon = should be level

teaspoon = should be level

ounce = in most of my recipes, the ounce measurement is approximate

handful = just that, a palmful of the ingredient in question...no exact measurement here

knob = a term used in England to denote an amount of butter. I imagine it to be a heaped tablespoon...perhaps a little more? Do not concern yourself with being exact (unless I ask you to be)—a knob or two of butter will not hurt your dish.

* pans (and pots)—I only use non-stick pans with tight-fitting lids. The one item that I suggest that you invest in is a deep stockpot—this will be useful when preparing "dal" (lentils, beans, and pulses) in large amounts. My own pot holds 8 quarts.

* spoons—I only use wooden spoons as they will not scratch my non-stick pans.

* heat/flame level—I refer to low/medium/high flames and some levels in between. Each stove and oven performs to its own tune so until you are confident that you have found the level that I am speaking of, please keep your eye upon whatever is cooking. My suggestion will vary slightly in each home.

* recipe yield—you might ask why the recipe yields more than two to three servings. Well, my theory is that if the dish freezes well, lasts for a day or two, and as you are going to the effort anyway, why not make enough for two dinners or a frozen meal for next week? However, if you choose to halve the yield, simply halve the ingredients and the recipe should still work. The same holds true if you are to double the amounts.

* spice level—see the section on "Spices and Herbs." If you need to omit or lessen a spice, just do it. I urge you to make a note of the adjustment in your recipe book as soon as you taste the delicious, finished product and you are sure that you were successful. This way, you will be certain to create the very same (or close to it) the next time you prepare it. My recipe will give you a place from which to start—I assure you that if you follow it, you will attain a most satisfying result, but do keep in mind that there are no strict rules. Allow yourself some inconsistencies. I have made my mum's recipes, *my* own. Now you should make my recipes, *your* own.

Like many, I grew up being told that textbooks are precious and not to be dog-eared or written in. While I savor my kitchen bibles, I openly encourage personal scratchings when it comes to a favored recipe book. You will come across yellow post-it notes, turned-down corners, and my own handwriting strewn over the method in the cookbooks that I frequent most regularly. Sometimes I tamper with a recipe or decide that I require more salt or that I had misinterpreted an instruction—if I jot it down, then and there, the finished plate is more likely to be expressly to my liking the next time I give it a shot. Go ahead, feel free to whip out your red pen.

YOUR NOTES...

MASALA 1

"Masala" means a blend of spices. It may be a raw, dry spice mix or in this case, a cooked paste. This recipe requires a little time and some effort (namely—pulling out, using, washing, and putting away the food processor), but it is worth it. A well-cooked masala (or sauce/base for your recipe) will cement your dish and make it a winner. My mum habitually makes a huge batch and freezes individual portions; these really are a lifesaver when you want to cook an additional dish but think that doing so may just throw you over the edge—you have already done the hard work. I am presenting one portion size in this recipe, and I will tell you when and how to use it in later recipes. Make it, freeze it, reach for it.

Preparation time: 10 minutes
Cooking time: 45–50 minutes
Notes: Use as a base for later recipes (I will tell you where).
Serving suggestion: N/A
M/A: Yes. I make up to 3 days in advance.
* Yes

2	medium-sized onions, quartered
3"–4"	piece of fresh ginger, peeled
3–4	cloves of garlic (optional)
4	tablespoons canola oil
1	teaspoon salt
1	tablespoon garam masala
1	tablespoon turmeric
1	teaspoon red chili powder
1–2	black cardamoms (optional, cracked open)
1	cup chopped/crushed tomatoes (canned is ideal for this)
2	cups boiling water—and possibly a little more

- Place the onions, ginger, and garlic in a food processor. Pulse for 2–3 minutes until a smooth(ish) paste results.

- Heat the oil in a frying pan, over a medium flame, for a minute or so.

- Now, add the contents of the food processor to the pan and cook for 5–7 minutes while stirring occasionally—do not allow to burn.

- Add the salt and spices. Stir and cook in the same way for a further 3–4 minutes.

- Pour in the crushed tomatoes, turn the heat to medium/high, stir regularly, and cook for about 10 minutes.

- Add the boiling water, combine the contents of the pan, bring to a boil for a minute, turn the heat to low/medium, and put the lid on the pan. Allow to cook for 25–30 minutes—mix intermittently and add $^1/_2$–1 cup of boiling water at a time to retain the consistency (it should resemble the texture of a salsa).

Done. The time-consuming part is complete.

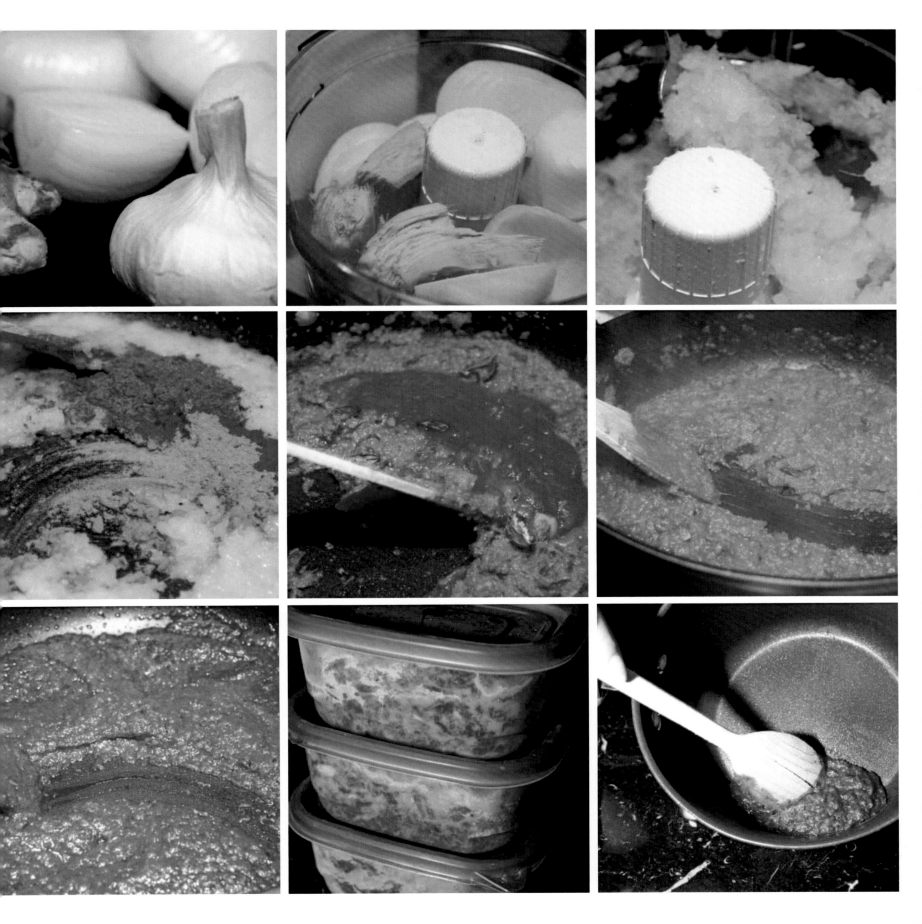

MASALA 2

This is an important "base" to learn to create—from this you can conjure up many "dals" (lentils) and meat dishes. In some recipes, only half of this masala is called for—freeze the other half and pull out when in a hurry. You will have a robust and flavorful starting point for something more—much more. I will tell you when and how to use this recipe later. FYI, as regards flavor it is very similar to Masala 1 (previous page) but it takes less time to cook and texturally it is chunkier.

Preparation time: 5–10 minutes
Cooking time: 25–30 minutes
Notes: Use as a base for later recipes (I will tell you where).
Serving suggestion: N/A
M/A: Yes. I make up to 3 days in advance.
* Yes

4	tablespoons canola oil
2	tablespoons cumin seeds
1	large onion, chopped
2	tablespoons ginger, grated
1	tablespoon salt
2	tablespoons garam masala
1	tablespoons turmeric
1	teaspoon red chili powder
1	black cardamom (optional, cracked open)
1	cup chopped/crushed tomatoes (canned is ideal for this)

- In a large frying pan, heat the oil over a medium flame for a minute or so.

- Add the cumin seeds, onions, and ginger. Combine and allow to soften for 5 minutes while stirring to prevent sticking.

- Spoon in all the spices, mix well, and cook for 8 minutes or so—do not allow to burn. Mix from time to time.

- Pour in the tomatoes, continue to mix regularly and cook for a further 10–12 minutes until a deep, rich, red/brown sauce evolves.

Done. Ready for the next step.

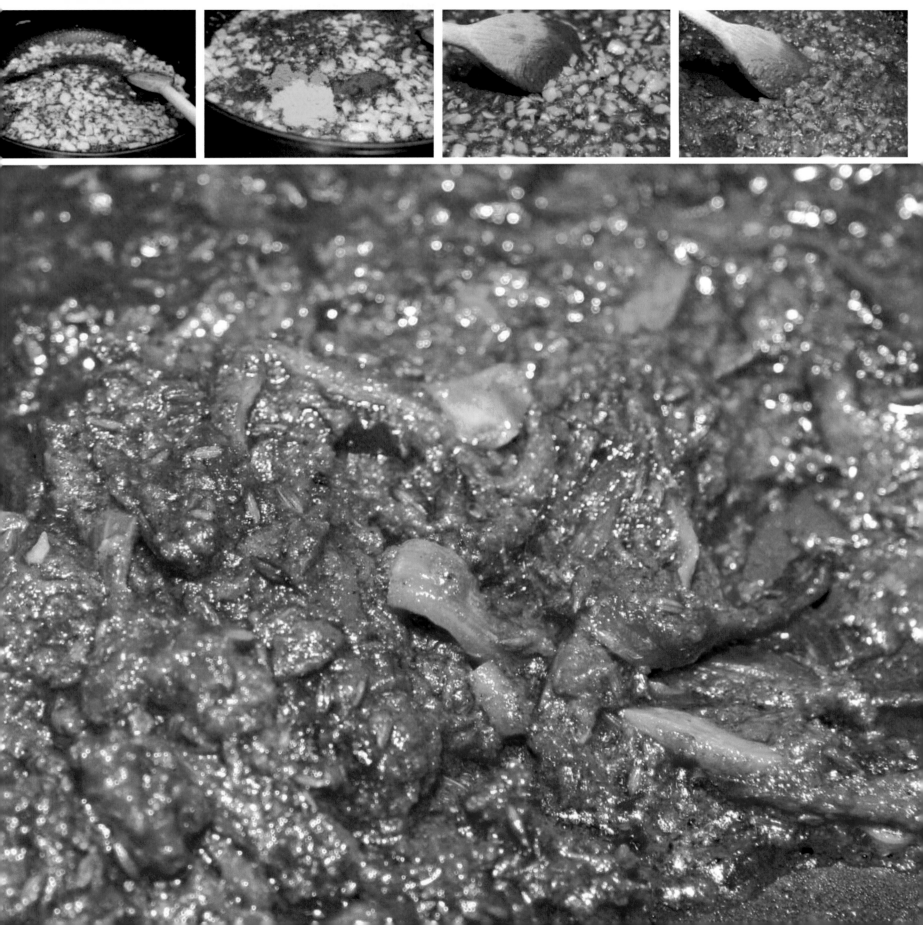

NIBBLES...

INDIAN FRIES

How to jazz up the ordinary French fry? With a simple seasoning...voila...you can create something extraordinary. My mum always carries a little Ziploc bag with her which contains a blend of these spices just in case she needs to "fix" something while eating out. As a child, the appearance of the bag in public used to make me cringe with embarrassment, but it also changed the way I ate fish and chips forever. (Oh...and nowadays I pride myself in concealing—and subsequently revealing—my own suspicious-looking stash.)

Serves: 2
Preparation time: 5–10 minutes
Cooking time: 10 minutes
Notes: I use white or yukon gold potatoes—I am not particularly fussy.
Use the same spices sprinkled over warm popcorn too.
Serving suggestion: With buttered bread and tomato ketchup or mayonnaise.
M/A: No. However, you can peel, slice, and steep the potatoes in water if you are not preparing them immediately. Drain and fry as below when you are ready to. Serve immediately.
* No

1	pound potatoes (see "Notes")
	canola oil—enough for deep-frying, about 3" deep
$^1/_2$	teaspoon salt
$^1/_2$	teaspoon garam masala
$^1/_4$	teaspoon red chili powder

- Peel, wash, and slice the potato lengthways into $^1/_2$" (approximately) fingers. Wash and then drain the potatoes well in a colander.

- Heat the oil over medium heat in a wok or deep pan.

- When the oil begins to bubble gently, test the temperature by adding an uncooked fry. If the addition of it creates more bubbles and the fry rises to the top of the pan, carefully add all of the potato fingers. If the fry browns almost immediately, the oil is too hot. Remove the fry and turn the heat down slightly.

- Wait for a few minutes and try again. If the potato sinks, the oil is too cold and you will have to remove the fry and reattempt in a few minutes. (I tell myself to be patient.)

- Using a slotted spoon, check to see when the fries become a golden color—it should take 4–5 minutes. Scoop the cooked fries into a dry colander.

- While the potato chips are still hot, sprinkle with the salt, garam masala, and chili powder—this way the seasoning sticks. Toss.

Done.

SPICY CHEESE ON TOAST

As a newlywed, this was the first breakfast that I ever awarded my husband. He could not keep his hands off it—the toast, not me! Effortless to prepare, it serves as a mighty hit whether it is a morning meal, appetizer, or side plate. As an alternative, use the spiced cheese to bring life to a baked potato, quesadilla, or omelet or for stuffing mushrooms before baking. Sanjay often asks for a "snack" between meals—it is perpetually this that he is referring to.

Serves: 4
Preparation time: 15–20 minutes
Cooking time: 5–10 minutes
Notes: Use smaller slices of bread, such as 1″ French bread rounds, for an hors d'oeuvre but have plenty as these will go fast.
Serving suggestion: With a salad for lunch or as is for a quick pick-me-up.
M/A: Yes. Prepare, refrigerate, and dip into the cheese mixture for up to 3 days. Broil as below when you are ready to. Serve straight away.
* No

3	cups grated sharp cheddar cheese
1/2	small red onion, chopped
1	jalapeno pepper, seeds/membranes removed, chopped
1	large tomato, chopped
	a large handful of cilantro, chopped
2	teaspoons garam masala
1	teaspoon red chili powder (optional)
8	slices (approximately) of any bread you choose (I use traditional sandwich bread or English muffins)

- Combine all of the ingredients except the bread in a mixing bowl. Taste test and adjust the seasoning if needed. Add more cheese if it is too spicy.

- Lightly toast both sides of the bread under the broiler on a foil-lined tray (easier cleanup).

- Evenly top the bread slices (right up to the edges) with the mixture. Place under the broiler until the cheese is bubbling and browning—about 3–4 minutes under medium heat. Keep an eye on them.

Done.

TURKEY BURGERS

These healthy burgers will get a nod from all. Make full-size burgers or mini-sliders as I have shown. Grilled kebabs on skewers work splendidly too. Serve the bread bun on the side for the sake of all the lo-carbers at your lunch or display the patty over a grilled portobello mushroom and dressed field greens. Dress up or keep it simple—naked or not (the burger)—you will be back for more. This recipe works well when wanting to introduce your children (or anyone for that matter) to Indian flavors...just omit the chili powder if your audience calls for it.

Serves: 4, if making quarter-pound burgers

Preparation time: 10 minutes

Cooking time: 10 minutes

Notes: I have used 99% fat-free turkey before and found that the burgers have a tendency to become dry. My recommendation is 90–94% lean turkey.

Use lamb or any other ground meat that appeals.

These burgers can be grilled or put under the broiler to prepare too.

You may double this recipe but stick to only 1 egg as more makes the mix difficult to manipulate.

Serving suggestion: Serve warm alongside sandwich buns and your favorite condiment. My choice would be a cucumber raita (see "Accompaniments" section).

M/A: Yes. Make the turkey mixture and refrigerate up to 24 hours ahead of time.

* Yes. Freeze the prepared turkey mix, remove when needed, thaw, mold into burgers, and cook as below.

1	pound ground turkey (see "Notes")
1	small red onion, very finely chopped
1	jalapeno pepper, seeds/membranes removed, very finely chopped
1	tablespoon fresh ginger, finely grated
	a large handful of cilantro, chopped
1	whole egg
1 1/2	teaspoons salt
1 1/2	tablespoons garam masala
3/4	teaspoon red chili powder
2	teaspoons cumin seeds
2	teaspoons pomegranate powder or mango powder
	canola oil—if frying, about 4 tablespoons

- Combine all of the ingredients, except the oil, in a bowl. Use your hands to mix well and evenly distribute all of the flavors.

- Heat a teaspoon of the oil in a frying pan. Take a tablespoon of the meat mixture, mold in your hands, and flatten into a small patty. Fry on both sides in the pan. Taste test the cooked patty to check for seasoning. Adjust the uncooked mixture as needed.

- Divide the mixture into 4 equal parts for larger burgers. Mold into 3/4–1″ thick rounds or into several smaller rounds for sliders (about 1/4 cup of the packed mixture will yield a traditional mini-slider and uniform size). If the meat is difficult to manage and appears to be sticky, coat your hands with a little canola oil and this will help. Place the burgers onto a foil-lined tray. Cover with foil and refrigerate for up to 24 hours but at least 1 hour for best results. (Remember, the egg is the only binder so cooling will allow the patties to better hold their shape during cooking. The flavors will have the opportunity to marry with the meat too.)

- Heat a little oil over low/medium heat in a shallow pan. Carefully place the burgers into the pan. Cook on both sides until ready (about 4–5 minutes per side).

Done.

PAKORAS (INDIAN TEMPURA)

While testing the recipe for these bites, I realized that I just do not make pakoras enough. This savory snack is a real treat for tea-time with chai (see "Drinks" section) or as an appetizer with a glass of chilled wine. They remind me of being at my grandmother's home. She would make them opting for potatoes and cauliflower, and the grandchildren would fight over the scraps of fried batter that were leftover in the bottom of the colander. You may be fighting too...

Serves: 4–6

Preparation time: 20 minutes + 30 minutes waiting time

Cooking time: approximately 5 minutes per batch

Notes: Double the batter mixture if you have a lot of vegetables to fry.

Be inventive—set up a fondue dinner.

Serving suggestion: Serve with mayonnaise, ketchup, or hot sauce. Mint chutney is a popular choice too (see "Accompaniments" section).

M/A: Yes. Prepare the batter up to 1 hour before needed, chop the vegetables, and then fry the pakoras when you are ready to.

* No

batter: (enough for approximately 2 pounds of chicken)

1 ½	cups gram flour
1 ½	teaspoons salt
1	tablespoon garam masala
1	teaspoon red chili powder
1	tablespoon pomegranate powder
1	tablespoon mango powder
2	tablespoons dried fenugreek leaves
½	teaspoon carom seeds
¾–1	cup cold water (approximately), to make a smooth batter

vegetable(s) of your choice:
    e.g., potato, cauliflower, eggplant rounds, spinach leaves, onion rings

or:

protein(s) of your choice:
    e.g., deveined shrimp, 1″ thick chicken or cod cubes

canola oil—enough for deep-frying, about 3″ deep

- Using a handheld whisk, combine the flour, the seasonings, and a little of the water at a time in a bowl. Whisk well. The batter should be smooth and lump-free. The batter should also coat the back of a spoon without running off. Cover and leave for at least 30 minutes as this allows the flavors to combine.

- Meanwhile, wash, dry, and slice the vegetables or the proteins of your choice. Slice uniformly to ensure all the pakoras cook evenly—about ¼″–½″ thickness. If using a protein, 1″ thickness will work.

- Heat the oil in a deep pan or wok. When the oil is beginning to bubble, dip the victim in the batter, allow the excess batter to drip off, and lower into the pan. Just do one, allow to brown, scoop up, drain in a colander or on paper towels, and taste test for salt and whether it is cooked through.

- Adjust the batter seasoning or oil temperature (turn down the flame slightly if the test piece is not cooked through).

- Now, continue to dip, drip, cook, drain.

Done.

KEEMA (GROUND LAMB)

This dish is as painless to prepare as it is impressive to serve. Traditionally the ground lamb ("keema") is served with chapattis (see "Breads" section) and raita (see "Accompaniments" section). I was hosting a book club one evening, and as so many of my friends were being "careful" before the summer holidays, I chose lettuce leaves as the wrap. It is comical how we readers appreciated the lighter version while washing it down (not so carefully) with plenty of laughs and Merlot! Wait, I do not think anyone would even recall the title of the book...

Serves: 6 as a main dish, 10 for lettuce wraps
Preparation time: 5 minutes
Cooking time: 30 minutes
Notes: If you cannot find ground lamb, ask your grocery store butcher to grind it for you.
Serving suggestion: Toss with cooked spaghetti for a real twist on the usual. I like to add a squeeze of fresh lemon juice too.
Wrap with hummus to make a delicious burrito.
How about a not so sloppy "Sloppy Joe"?
Tortilla chips layered with the lamb, sour cream, and guacamole is always a winning alternative to the traditional. I have also shown you how to make spring rolls with the keema as a filling on the following page.
M/A: Yes. Just heat before serving.
* Yes

4	tablespoons canola oil
1	medium onion, finely chopped or finely sliced
2	tablespoons fresh ginger, grated
2	tablespoons cumin seeds
2 ½	teaspoons salt
2	tablespoons garam masala
1	tablespoon turmeric
1 ½	teaspoons red chili powder
2	pounds ground lamb
1	pound frozen peas

- Heat the oil in a big, shallow pan—you will need a large surface area.

- Add the cumin seeds, onion, and ginger. Stir and cook over medium heat until the onions are translucent—about 5–7 minutes.

- Add the salt, garam masala, turmeric, and chili powder. Allow the spices to cook for 2–3 minutes.

- Place the lamb in the pan and—using a wooden spoon—keep mixing while breaking the meat into smaller pieces. Turn up the heat to medium/high. Browning and cooking the lamb will take about 20 minutes. (This may become tedious.)

- At this point, stir in the frozen peas and cook for a further 5 minutes.

- **Done.**

SPRING ROLLS...

As well as affording one the opportunity to make use of cooked leftovers, they serve as a popular appetizer. Whichever filling you choose to use, it should be quite dry—I mean not "saucy"—or else you will have soggy rolls, and those are never tempting. I use the mini ready-made, store-bought wonton wraps (they are usually found in the refrigerated section of the grocery store). Read the instructions carefully and then just follow what I tell you. Easy.

Taking 1 tablespoon of filling (at room temperature), form a sausage-shape between two corners of the laid out wrapper.

Fold in the back flap and wrap over the meat—lightly press down with your thumb as you bring in the two side corners.

Holding down all three corners, tuck in the filling and roll gently but firmly towards the last flap. Dab the corner with some eggwash (whisked egg) and "stick" down the final corner.

Place, fold-side down, on a plate until you are ready to fry. (I refrigerate for 4 or 5 hours before a dinner party.)

Deep-fry in hot canola oil until golden brown for 3–4 minutes (test one roll first to check for the correct temperature of the oil—if the roll browns too quickly, turn the heat down slightly). Drain on a paper towel and serve piping hot with chili sauce or aioli if you prefer. **Done.**

Paneer bhurji or alloo, sukhe are other perfect choices for fillings (see "Vegetables" section).

AVOCADO TOASTS

Mash the flesh of a **ripe avocado** with overly generous pinches of **salt**, **black pepper**, and **mango powder**—spread over **mini toasts**. Drizzle with **olive oil** (optional and not a common ingredient of the Indian kitchen) and sprinkle with **chili flakes** for an immediate and eye-catching appetizer. **Done.**

SPICY BEANS ON TOAST

This twist on the popular British staple reminds me of my uncle. When he visits from India, this is his breakfast of choice each and every morning. My mum takes extra care of him by topping it with a fried egg and a splash of Tabasco sauce...as big sisters do.

Serves: 2
Preparation time: 5 minutes
Cooking time: 10 minutes
Notes: I would not choose maple syrup flavored beans—I find them to be too sweet.
Serving suggestion: Serve hot, over buttered toast. Also a great filling for a baked potato.
M/A: Yes. Just heat before serving.
* No

2	tablespoons canola oil
1	small onion, finely chopped
1/2	jalapeno pepper, finely chopped
1/2	teaspoon salt
1	teaspoon garam masala
1/4	teaspoon red chili powder
1	can baked beans in tomato sauce —approximately 14 ounces
	a handful of cilantro, chopped
	bread and butter—to serve

- Heat the oil in a pan for a minute or so and add the onions—soften and brown over low heat for 4–5 minutes.

- Add the jalapeno pepper, salt, and spices. Mix for 1 minute as the spices cook.

- Pour in the baked beans, stir, and heat through for 3–4 minutes. (I usually drain off and discard a little of the tomato sauce before I add to the pan—it is just a matter of taste.)

- Throw in the cilantro and combine.

  Done.

CARROT, GINGER, AND CILANTRO SOUP

I have taken my friend's recipe and (with her permission) slightly tampered with it. She is an enviable home-chef, dinner hostess, and businesswoman. How does she do it? Never mind that right now...this spot-hitting soup is our immediate concern. It is one of the most raved-about recipes at my classes as it is undemanding of the cook yet presents amazing results. A reminder to myself—sometimes the simple way is the best way.

Serves: 8
Preparation time: 10 minutes
Cooking time: 50 minutes
Notes: Use a 2-pound bag of pre-peeled, baby carrots—much easier than peeling your own.
If you find the soup to be too spicy, add a little extra milk.
Serving suggestion: This soup is a treat when chilled too—I have offered it this way in shot glasses.
(M/A): Yes.
* Yes

3	tablespoons canola oil
1	medium onion, sliced
2–3	tablespoons fresh ginger, coarsely grated
1/2	small jalapeno, roughly chopped (optional)
2	pounds carrots, peeled, roughly chopped into 2″ pieces
1	teaspoon salt
1/2	teaspoon black pepper
4	cups boiling water
2–3	cups milk (I use 2%)
	a handful of cilantro, finely chopped

- In a deep pan, heat the oil over medium heat for a minute or so.

- Add the onion and ginger and cook for 8–10 minutes until softened. Stir regularly to hinder burning. Adjust heat if need be.

- Mix in the jalapeno, carrots, salt, and pepper. Continue to stir for 2–3 minutes.

- Pour in the boiling water, bring to a boil, and then pop on the lid and simmer over medium heat for 40–45 minutes or so; using a fork, check that the carrots are tender before moving on.

- Using a handheld, electric blender (or transfer to a countertop blender), blend to a smooth puree.

- Pour in the milk (the amount depends upon your desired consistency) and heat through over a medium flame.

- Stir in the cilantro before serving.

Done.

ALLOO TIKKI (POTATO PATTIES)

Tikkis are an authentic street food served on the roadsides of India. They will be fried before your eyes by a street vendor, drizzled with tamarind sauce, and presented to you on a banyan leaf. I grace mine upon the first plate I grab and adorn with a good old squirt of tomato ketchup. Although not commonly served in this manner, consider topping with a poached egg—bathing my crispy tikki (and all of its even crispier protrusions) with a warm, gooey yolk has rewarded me with a breakfast like never before.

Serves: 10 (makes about 20 patties)
Simply halve the recipe for a smaller yield.
Preparation time: 80–90 minutes
Cooking time: 5 minutes per batch
Notes: I use white or yukon gold potatoes.
Begin with the potatoes (approximately 3 pounds). Put into a large pan with enough water to cover the potatoes. Bring the water to a boil, cover the pot with a tight-fitting lid, turn the heat to low/medium, and allow to simmer for about 55–60 minutes until the potatoes are cooked through. A knife should easily slide through the middle of the potato. Check that there is enough water to cover the potatoes as they cook and add more if need be. Remove from the heat. Drain in a colander until cool. The peel should scrape off easily—discard. Grate into a large bowl or use a potato ricer if you have one—I do not have one, and therefore, the grater is just fine.
Serving suggestion: Bread and your favorite condiment. As a traditional samosa (pastry triangle similar to spanakopita) filling.

3	pounds potatoes (approximately)—peeled, boiled, drained, grated finely (see "Notes")
2	teaspoons salt
2	tablespoons garam masala
1	teaspoon red chili powder
1	tablespoon mango powder
1	medium onion, red or white, very finely chopped
2	tablespoons fresh ginger, grated finely
1–2	jalapeno peppers, finely chopped (optional)
	a really large handful of cilantro, chopped
1	cup frozen peas, allow to defrost for 20 minutes or so in a colander
2	cups all-purpose flour
	canola oil—for deep-frying, about 3″ deep

M/A: Yes. Prepare as below. Drain on paper towels. Pop in oven and heat through before serving.
* No

- Using your hands and a large mixing bowl, combine all of the ingredients (except the flour and oil) well. Taste test the mix and adjust accordingly—you may require more salt.

- Make the potato patties about 2 ¹/₂″ in diameter and 1″ thick (about ¹/₄ cup of the packed mixture will yield a traditional and uniform size). It is important to pack the potato mixture tightly when forming the patties or else they may fall apart during frying. Rub your hands with a little canola oil to prevent the mix from sticking to your hands while forming the tikki if need be.

- Put flour on a flat plate. Roll each patty in the flour, dust off, and arrange on a clean plate before frying.

- Heat the oil in a wok or other deep pan. Deep-fry one patty to check the oil temperature and that the potato is heated through. Fry the rest of the tikkis in batches and take care not to overcrowd the pan as this will cause the temperature to drop—about 4 or 5 tikkis at a time is good. It should take about 4–5 minutes per batch. Turn the tikki carefully once during frying.

- Drain on paper towels.

Done.

EGG BHURJI (SCRAMBLED EGGS)

Your guests will forever remember this addition to your brunch. It is intriguing, has a kick to it, and is simple to pull together. It can satisfy a call for breakfast, lunch, or a light supper. I have never made these eggs with the whites only but give it a go if you feel it is the right thing to do. Share with bread or make a rolled tortilla with the eggs, salsa, and sour cream—you may as well include the egg yolks if you are doing the latter. Just marvelous.

Serves: 3–4
Preparation time: 10 minutes
Cooking time: 10 minutes
Notes: The same recipe makes a superb omelet or spicy quiche filling.
Serving suggestion: With toast and anything else that goes with traditional scrambled eggs.
M/A: No. However, you can cook the onions and ginger and put aside. Beat the eggs and seasoning and refrigerate beforehand too. Scramble as below when you are ready to.
* No

3	tablespoons canola oil
1	small onion, finely sliced
1	tablespoon fresh ginger, grated
8	eggs
1	teaspoon salt
2	teaspoons garam masala
$1/2$	teaspoon red chili powder
$1/2$–1	jalapeno pepper, chopped
	a handful of cilantro, chopped

- Heat the oil in a frying pan. Add the onion and ginger and brown lightly over a medium flame for 5 minutes. Stir occasionally to prevent burning.

- Meanwhile, crack the eggs into a bowl. Add the salt, spices, jalapeno pepper, and cilantro. Beat with a fork.

- Pour the egg mixture over the onions and ginger. Let set for 1 minute in the pan.

- Now, scramble gently, using a wooden spoon. This will take 3–4 minutes.

Done.

FISH KOFTAS

This recipe evolved one afternoon when I was hopelessly searching the fridge for a dinner idea. There were only last night's leftover salmon and mashed potatoes visible, but by adding a few staples, a yummy fishcake was created. There are no exact amounts here...it is leftovers—so make this recipe your own.

Serves: 4
Preparation time: 10–15 minutes
Cooking time: 10 minutes
Notes: No leftovers? Buy ready-cooked salmon and mashed potatoes from your local deli.
Serving suggestion: With your favorite condiment. I like mint chutney (see "Accompaniments" section).
M/A: No. However, you can mold into rounds and cook just before serving.
* No

2	salmon fillets, cooked
2	cups mashed potatoes (approximately)
1	small red onion, finely chopped
1	jalapeno pepper, finely chopped (optional)
	a handful of cilantro, chopped
1	tablespoon garam masala
1	tablespoon mango powder
$^1/_2$	teaspoon salt (if you need it)
1	egg
3–4	tablespoons canola oil

- Using a fork, flake the salmon into a large bowl. Discard the skin.

- Add all the other ingredients except the egg and salt and mix well. Steal a taste to test for seasoning. Remember that the fish and potatoes are probably already seasoned so be cautious. Adjust to taste and add the salt if needed.

- Crack open an egg and mix all the ingredients together using your fingers.

- Take approximately 1 heaped tablespoon of the mix and roll into small rounds and place onto a foil-lined tray. If the mixture appears difficult to handle, rub a little canola oil over your hands before molding. Cover and refrigerate for at least an hour before cooking. This will allow the balls to hold their shape better while browning.

- Heat the oil in a frying pan over low/medium heat for a minute or so.

- Carefully place the fish balls in the pan. Stir gently—this will only take 5–7 minutes as the main ingredients are already cooked. Just heat through and brown.

Done.

SEASONED NUTS

The aroma of these nuts and spices being prepared over the stove will have you reaching in and risking burnt fingers. Allow the nuts to cool, pour a glass of whatever the time of day dictates, and indulge. My dad relaxes munching on these while nursing his Scotch and watching the evening news—minute pleasures but the ones I yearn to see and be a part of the most.

Serves: 8–10 with drinks
Preparation time: No time
Cooking time: 5–8 minutes
Notes: Use unsalted nuts, one type or a mixture is fine—you choose. I often do a blend of almonds, cashews, pecan halves, and pistachio nuts.
Serving suggestion: Alongside a wedge of Brie, some prosciutto, and sliced apples.
M/A: Yes. Store in an airtight container for up to one week. They taste super when cool too so make them a day or two ahead of your dinner party.
* No

2 ¹/₂	tablespoons canola oil
	unsalted almonds/cashew nuts—total of 1 pound
1 ¹/₄	teaspoons salt
2	teaspoons black pepper
1	tablespoon mango powder
¹/₂	teaspoon red chili powder (optional)

- Heat the oil over medium heat in a non-stick frying pan for a minute or so.

- Add the nuts, keep stirring for 6–7 minutes. Do not allow them to burn.

- When the nuts begin to turn golden brown, add the salt, black pepper, and mango powder. Stir well for 2 minutes. Try to ensure that the spices are well distributed. Taste a nut to check for salt and add a little more if need be—best done while the nuts are still in the hot pan.

- Spread the seasoned nuts on a large tray, allow to cool, and then store or eat warm if you cannot possibly wait.

  Done.

CREAMED MUSHROOMS

This is a variation on the British version of creamed mushrooms. If you had any doubts, I hope you will concede and see just how manageable it is to spin an Indian twist on any one of your favorites. Add a touch of elegance to your brunch by loading mini croissants with the mushrooms, wrapping in foil, and heating in the oven for a few minutes. Alternatively, serve on toast or in a crepe with a mimosa for an unforgettable breakfast.

Serves: 4–6
Preparation time: 10 minutes
Cooking time: 15 minutes
Serving suggestion: Over toast or as a filling for croissants, a baked potato, crepe, or an omelet.
M/A: No. However, you can prepare as below and stop just before adding the cream. Add the cream and heat through just before serving. I say this as I have found that when not eaten immediately, my leftovers turn a miserable shade of gray. Still gratifying—just gray!
* No

3	tablespoons canola oil
1	medium onion, very finely chopped
1	tablespoon cumin seeds
1	teaspoon salt
2	teaspoons garam masala
1	pound mushrooms (baby, oyster, shitake, or a mix), sliced/chopped
3/4	cup heavy cream
	a handful of cilantro, chopped

- Heat the oil over low heat in a large non-stick frying pan for a minute or so.

- Add the onions and cumin seeds. Turn the heat to medium. Allow the onions to become translucent—it takes about 4–5 minutes while stirring.

- Fold in the mushrooms and cook until golden—it will take another 4–5 minutes.

- Mix in the salt and garam masala. Cook for 2–3 minutes.

- Pour in the cream and heat through for a further 2–3 minutes.

- Toss in the cilantro and stir well.

Done.

SALMON CARPACCIO

Serves: 6
Preparation time: 15 minutes
Cooking time: N/A
Notes: There are no definite measurements for this one—simply add more or less of an ingredient at your will.
Serving suggestion: On an elegant appetizer spoon or on mini toasts.
M/A: No. However you can prepare the dressing earlier and add the salmon when you are ready to serve.
* No

- In a mixing bowl, whisk together:

1	tablespoon canola oil
1	teaspoon finely grated ginger
1/4	teaspoon black pepper
1/2	teaspoon ground cumin
	the juice of half a large lemon
1	tablespoon cilantro, finely chopped
1	jalapeno pepper, de-seeded and finely chopped (optional)

- Now, gently fold in:

1/2	diced mango (approximately)
14–16	ounces smoked salmon, chopped (approximately)
	a pinch of salt (if you need it)

Done.

TURKEY WITH A "TWEAK"

My mum has to order the biggest Christmas turkey in the neighborhood, and I am sure it is just so that she can put her applauded spin on the ample leftovers. Actually, all of my aunties do exactly the same. However, you do not have to wait until Thanksgiving or December 25—just use a store-bought rotisserie chicken as I often do.

Remove the meat and discard the bones, skin, and any yucky bits. Melt **a knob of butter** with **a little canola oil.** Estimate your amounts here—add **cumin seeds**, **salt**, **garam masala**, **red chili powder (optional)**, and **pomegranate powder** to taste and cook the spices for 2–3 minutes. Mix in the chicken or turkey. Allow the poultry to brown and heat through. **Done.**

Squeeze some **lemon juice** *over (a must) and grab a fork.*

(You might also think about making a sandwich with your "tweaked" turkey, favorite bread, lettuce, and mayonnaise.)

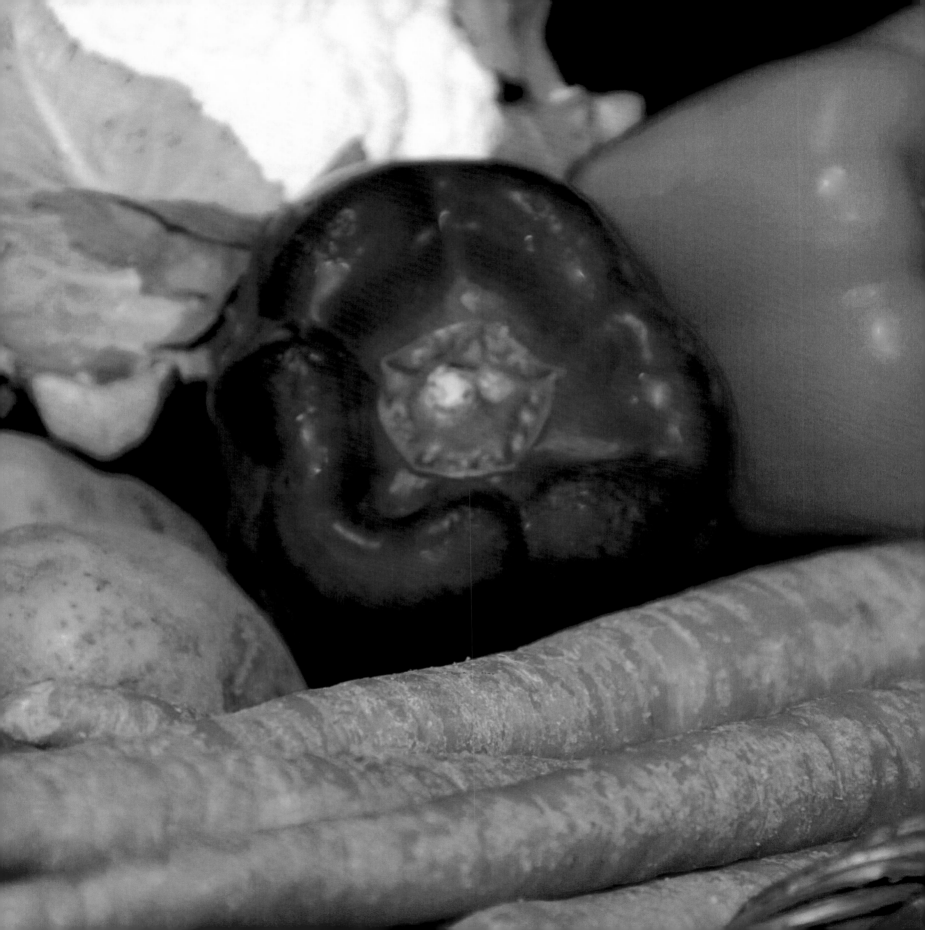

VEGETABLES...

PALAAK PANEER (SPINACH AND CHEESE)

Palaak paneer is a prized choice of mine and a hugely typical and popular dish with most Indian food lovers. It is a mighty source of both iron and protein so do not be put off by this dish's appearance—you will not be disappointed.

Serves: 6 as a side dish
Preparation time: 15 minutes
Cooking time: 40 minutes
Notes: If you have not used "paneer" before, learn a little about it in the "Commonly Used Ingredients" section.
At the time of pureeing the spinach leaves, I occasionally add a hefty knob of butter and ½ cup of heavy/double/whipping cream if I am feeling indulgent and want a "richer" finish.
Serving suggestion: With chapattis (see "Breads" section) and I have offered a pizza idea on the following page.
M/A: Yes. However, add the paneer to the cooked spinach just before serving (especially if you are having dinner guests) as the cheese is prone to crumble if too soft.
* Yes—without the paneer in it. Add the paneer and heat through just as you are planning to serve.

3	tablespoons canola oil
1	medium onion, sliced
1	tablespoon cumin seeds
1	tablespoon fresh ginger, grated
1	teaspoon salt
2	teaspoons garam masala
2	teaspoons turmeric
½	teaspoon red chili powder
2	tomatoes, sliced **OR** 1 cup chopped/crushed tomatoes (canned is ideal here)
2	bags spinach—approximately 9 ounces each, washed and drained
8–12	ounce (approximately) paneer cubes, any size (fresh or frozen, raw or fried)

- Heat the oil in a large, deep pan and add the onion, cumin seeds, and ginger. Cook over medium heat for 5 minutes or so. Stir regularly so it does not burn.

- Add the salt, garam masala, turmeric, and chili powder, mix well, and cook for another 2–3 minutes—do not burn.

- Now put in the tomatoes and allow the contents of the pan to blend and cook together for a further 8–10 minutes. Stir occasionally.

- Lay the spinach leaves over the tomato mixture. Cover the pan. (If all the leaves do not fit, add more gradually as the leaves cook and wilt down). Allow to cook, remembering to stir the contents every 3–4 minutes. This should take 15–20 minutes.

- Using a handheld, electric blender, cream the spinach into a smooth puree (just do this in the pan itself) and cook for 5 more minutes or feel free not to blend and to leave in its wilder state.

- Fold in the paneer and heat through for 10 minutes (taste a piece of paneer to determine that it is no longer frozen before serving).

Done.

I tasted a version of this recipe at a restaurant in New York a few years ago. I was intrigued by the thought of adding Punjabi flavors to an everyday staple.

*Use leftover **palaak paneer** (see previous page) to top **a store-bought pizza base**. If all of the cheese has been eaten, do not fret, improvise by arranging **crumbles of goat cheese** over the spinach and bake.*

I am slightly anemic, so I take immense pleasure and satisfaction in convincing myself that consuming a spinach-rich pizza—yes, the whole pizza—is all about taking proper care of myself.

Simply Radhika...

a traditional yet modern approach to my North Indian table

Radhika Behl

Thank you for purchasing

Simply Radhika...

Continue to support Radhika
by leaving a review on

amazon.com

PANEER BHURJI (SCRAMBLED CHEESE)

This is a substantial dish that is as beautiful to look at as it is fulfilling to eat. I have offered serving suggestions so just choose and know that this will become a regular at your table. Look at the plate—it is singing for you.

Serves: 6–8 as a side dish
Preparation time: 5–7 minutes
Cooking time: 25 minutes
Notes: If you have not used "paneer" before, learn a little about it in the "Spices and Herbs" section.
Serving suggestions: We serve it with chapattis (see "Breads" section) and dal (see "Lentils" section) but it is equally delicious when tucked into a pita pocket if a portable lunch is called for.
Look over the page for some additional ideas.
M/A: Yes. Just heat before serving or eat at room temperature.
* No

3	tablespoons canola oil
1	medium onion, sliced
1	tablespoon cumin seeds
1	large tomato, sliced
1	teaspoon salt
2	teaspoons garam masala
2	teaspoons turmeric
$1/2$	teaspoon red chili powder
1	pound bag frozen mixed vegetables
12	ounces (approximately) paneer (fresh or frozen and defrosted—crumbled)

- Heat the oil over low/medium heat in a frying pan. Add the onions and cumin seeds and cook for 5 minutes—do not allow to burn.

- Mix in the tomato and the spices. Cook for a further 5–7 minutes over a medium flame. Mix from time to time.

- Pour in the frozen mixed vegetables. Stir, cover, and allow to cook for 10 more minutes. Stir every now and then.

- Crumble in the paneer. Heat through for 4–5 minutes (taste a piece of paneer to be sure that it is warmed through).

  Done.

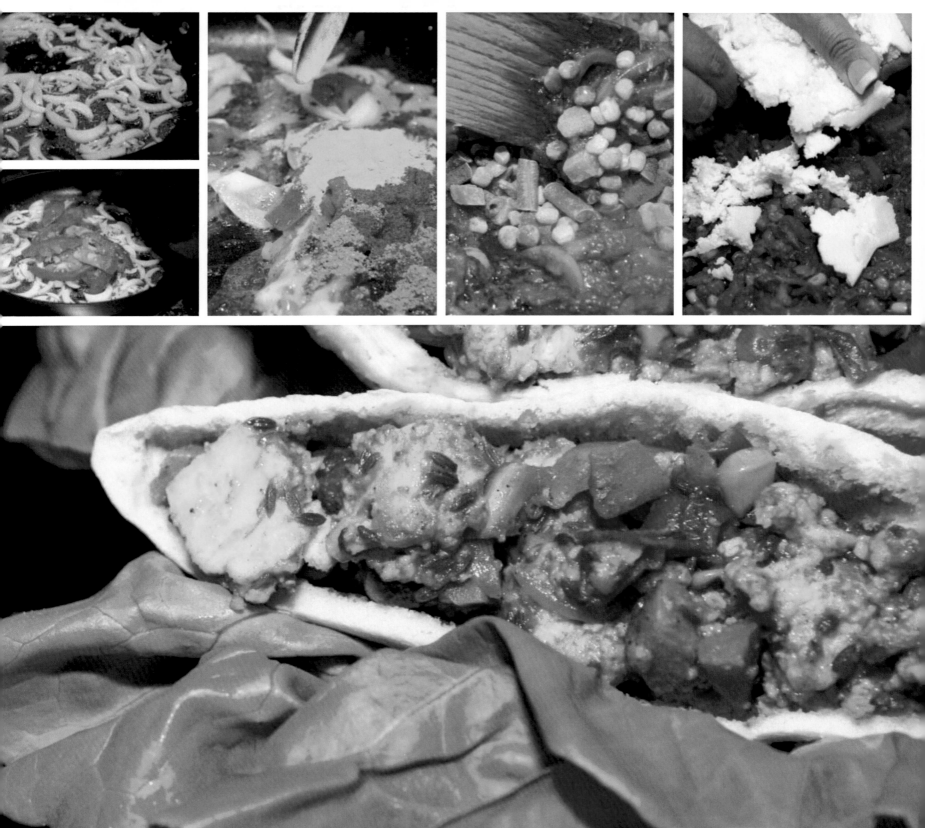

PANEER BHURJI—leftovers...

One of my best friends introduced me to these fabulous pastry wheels. She flavors hers with basil and feta cheese and made two hundred for my husband's fortieth birthday. A true friend indeed. I have altered the filling. Either way...a sure winner.

Serves: It depends upon what you have leftover. The full paneer bhurji recipe and 4 sheets of pastry should yield 32–36 wheels.
Preparation time: 15 minutes
Cooking time: 15 minutes
Notes: Keema recipe (see "Nibbles" section) works well in place of the paneer bhurji too.
Serving suggestion: As they are.
M/A: Yes, if eating at room temperature. Making 2–3 hours before serving works perfectly well.
* No

	paneer bhurji recipe (previous page)
	puff pastry, ready-made sheets (find in frozen section of grocery store)
1	egg, beaten (eggwash)

- Roll out the thawed pastry sheets (follow the instructions on the packet).

- Lay the paneer bhurji on top of a sheet.

- Roll into a log. Press the long end of the pastry sheet down firmly.

- Slice into wheels (about 1 $^1/_2$" thick) and place on a foil-lined baking tray.

- Brush the top of the wheel with beaten egg.

- Put the tray in the middle of a pre-heated oven (350°F) for 11–15 minutes or until golden.

  Done.

Serve the paneer bhurji with crisp endive leaves. The sharp contrast between the bitter leaf, the sweetness of the cooked carrot, and the smooth cheese crumbles creates a most memorable mouthful.

One of my go-to places to eat in Atlanta is a Persian restaurant—I frequent it all too often. Seasoned vegetables and meat kebabs alongside a selection of exotic rice dishes are the pull for its regulars. I have tried to interpret and play with one such rice dish.

Gently mix the warm **paneer bhurji** and freshly made **white rice** (see "Rice" section)—use a fork so as not to break up the grains. If both components are warm, the Indian spices will easily be absorbed by the rice. Throw in some **freshly grated orange zest**, **pine nuts**, **pistachios**, **raisins**, and **a little sugar**. Fluff with the fork once again. Cover the pan and allow the flavors to marry and the raisins to swell. Wait 10 minutes and dive in.

There are no exact measurements for this one—make it your own.

SUND (GINGER CURRY)

This somewhat "assertive" ginger sauce is customarily enjoyed during the winter months (or if one develops a cold, as it speaks loudly to the sinuses). I have shown you how to serve just a little sauce over the eggs so that you will still get all of the flavor of the ginger and not the pungency. In large quantities, sund may be too rich and for most it is an acquired taste, but I still urge you to try it. A new slant on "deviled eggs."

Serves: 8 as a side dish, 4 as a main dish
Preparation time: 5–10 minutes + time for boiling eggs
Cooking time: 20 minutes
Notes: I have offered two options to prepare below. The second option is the more traditional way to eat sund.
Serving suggestion: Over white rice (see "Rice" section) or alongside your favorite bread.
M/A: Yes. Just heat through and add the boiled eggs before serving.
* Yes. When I have some extra ginger in the fridge, I make this recipe and freeze it (without the extra water—second option).

2	tablespoons salted butter
2	tablespoons canola oil
1	tablespoon cumin seeds
¹/₂	cup fresh ginger, coarsely grated
1	teaspoon salt
1	tablespoon garam masala
1	tablespoon turmeric
¹/₂	teaspoon red chili powder
1	tablespoon mango powder
2	tablespoons dried fenugreek leaves
1	cup chopped/crushed tomatoes (canned is great in this instance)
	a handful of cilantro, chopped—to garnish
8	hard-boiled eggs—to serve

FOR SECOND OPTION:

2	cups boiling water (approximately)

- Melt the butter in a non-stick saucepan, add the oil and the cumin seeds, and heat over a low/medium flame for 2 minutes.

- Combine the ginger with the contents of the pan, stir every few minutes to prevent sticking, and continue for 7–8 minutes. (The ginger should become golden in color, and the aroma will be quite amazing.)

- Mix in the salt, garam masala, turmeric, red chili powder, mango powder, and fenugreek leaves. Reduce the heat to low and cook the spices for 2–3 minutes—do not allow to burn.

- Pour in the chopped tomatoes, stir, and cover the pan. Allow to simmer for 5 minutes so that all the flavors blend well.

Done.

1. Spoon over sliced, hard-boiled eggs and garnish with cilantro.

OR...

2. Add 2 cups of boiling water (more or less) to achieve a looser consistency. When all is combined and bubbling hot, add whole boiled eggs and serve egg curry over white rice for a truly hearty main meal.

ALLOO GAJAR (POTATOES AND CARROTS)

One day while nibbling on French bread and cream cheese, I reached for some of last night's leftovers. The combination of these three simple flavors is quite enviable.

Serves: 4 as a side dish
Preparation time: 15 minutes
Cooking time: 45 minutes
Notes: I use white or yukon gold potatoes—I am not really fussy.
Use a bag of baby, peeled carrots—make life easy.
Serving suggestion: With your favorite bread.
M/A: Yes. Just heat before serving.
* No

3	tablespoons canola oil
1	tablespoon cumin seeds
1	teaspoon salt
1	teaspoon garam masala
1	teaspoon turmeric
1/4	teaspoon red chili powder
1	pound carrots, diced into 1/2" cubes
1	pound potatoes, peeled and diced into 1/2" cubes (see "Notes")
	a handful of cilantro, chopped—to garnish

- Heat the oil in a non-stick, shallow frying pan over a low/medium flame.

- Add the cumin seeds and cook for 1 minute.

- Stir in the salt, garam masala, turmeric, and chili powder and cook the spices for 2 minutes—do not allow to burn.

- Add the carrots and coat well with oil. Cover the pan and leave for 5 minutes. Stir at intervals to prevent sticking.

- Add the potatoes, mix to coat with the spices, cover, and cook for a further 15–20 minutes. Stir every 5 minutes or so until both the vegetables are cooked through. If the vegetables begin to catch the bottom of the pan, add an additional 1–2 tablespoons of oil at this point.

- Switch off the heat and keep covered for a further 15 minutes or so.

Done.

ALLOO BEANS (POTATOES AND GREEN BEANS)

If someone in your family tends to shy from the French/green/runner bean—try this. Do not be fooled by the short list of ingredients—it is habitually a winner.

Serves: 4 as a side dish
Preparation time: 15 minutes
Cooking time: 45 minutes
Notes: I use white or yukon gold potatoes—I am not really fussy.
If you forget to buy the beans, double the amount of potatoes.
Serving suggestion: Chapattis (see "Breads" section) and moong dal (see "Lentils" section).
M/A: Yes. Just heat before serving.
* No

3	tablespoons canola oil
1	tablespoon cumin seeds
1	teaspoon salt
1	teaspoon garam masala
1	teaspoon turmeric
1/4	teaspoon red chili powder
1	pound French beans, chopped into 1" lengths
1	pound potatoes, peeled and diced into 1/2" cubes (see "Notes")

- Heat the oil in a non-stick, shallow frying pan over a low/medium flame.

- Add the cumin seeds and cook for 1 minute.

- Stir in the salt, garam masala, turmeric, and chili powder and cook spices for 2 minutes—do not allow to burn.

- Add the beans and coat well with the oil. Cover the pan and leave for 5 minutes. Stir at intervals to prevent sticking.

- Add the potatoes, mix to coat with the spices, cover, and cook for a further 15–20 minutes. Stir every 5 minutes or so until both the vegetables are cooked through. If the vegetables begin to catch the bottom of the pan, add an additional 1–2 tablespoons of oil at this point.

- Switch off the heat and keep covered for a further 15 minutes or so.

Done.

ALLOO GOBI (POTATOES AND CAULIFLOWER)

I find it difficult to control the amount of oil I use when cooking alloo gobi, and I invariably have to add more than I would like to prevent it from sticking to the base of the pan. Well...just add it—isn't a little yumminess better than none at all? This vegetable dish is a favorite of my dad. He believes no one makes it like his mum did. I can only dream that one day my son will say the same. For now, a "thank you, Mummy" will suffice.

Serves: 6–8 as a side dish
Preparation time: 10–15 minutes
Cooking time: 1 hour
Notes: I use white or yukon gold potatoes—I am not really fussy.
If you are able, wash the cauliflower the night before and allow it to drain. You are more likely to find a whole (not smashed) floret in your finished dish if the ingredient brings minimum water with it. Even with caution, this dish still has a tendency to become a mushy mess—no one but possibly you will notice.
Serving suggestion: With chapattis (see "Breads" section) and moong dal (see "Lentils" section).
M/A: Yes. Just heat before serving.
* No

5	tablespoons canola oil and probably some more
1	medium onion, finely sliced
1	tablespoon fresh ginger, grated
1	tablespoon cumin seeds
1 1/2	teaspoons salt
1	tablespoon garam masala
1	tablespoon turmeric
1/2	teaspoon red chili powder
1	cauliflower (approximately 1 1/2 pounds), cut into approximately 2″ florets
1	pound potatoes, peeled and cut into approximately 1 1/2″ cubes (see "Notes")
	a handful of cilantro, chopped—to garnish

- Heat the oil over a low/medium heat in a non-stick frying pan.

- Add the onions, ginger, and cumin seeds, stir, and cook until soft and the onions are translucent—this will take about 5–7 minutes.

- Stir in the salt, garam masala, turmeric, and chili powder. Cook the spices for 2–3 minutes—do not allow to burn.

- Mix in the cauliflower, coat well with the oil, and you will see that the florets quickly absorb the color of the turmeric. Cover the pan and allow to cook. Mix every few minutes and add 2 tablespoons of oil if you feel it catching the base of the pan or that there is not enough oil to coat the cauliflower. After about 15 minutes, the vegetable should be close to half-cooked.

- Add the potatoes, mix gently to distribute the onions, ginger, and cauliflower evenly. Cover. Mix from time to time. Add oil as required to prevent sticking. Cook until both the potatoes and the cauliflower are tender (it should be effortless to slide the tip of a knife into the cooked vegetables). This will take about 20–25 minutes and then turn off the heat and keep covered for a further 15 minutes or so.

Done.

ALLOO, THARI WALE (POTATO CURRY)

These scrumptious potatoes are traditionally eaten at lunchtime, and we would look forward to Sundays when my mum would often prepare them. It is simple, tasty, and most often served with pooris (see "Breads" section). Although not great for the waistline, it is altogether splendid and perfectly acceptable and desirable to indulge when followed by an afternoon nap. Mmm...

Serves: 6
Preparation time: 10 minutes
Cooking time: 35–40 minutes
Notes: I use white or yukon gold potatoes—I am not really fussy.
I am loosely referring to this dish as a "curry," indicating the Western notion of a deeply flavored "saucy" dish. You will notice that no curry powder (a commercially prepared mixture of spices) is used as most Indian homes do not utilize this ingredient.
Serving suggestion: With pooris (see "Breads" section) or over mattar pulau (see "Rice" section).
M/A: Yes. Just heat before serving.
* No

4	tablespoons canola oil
1	medium onion, finely sliced
1	tablespoon fresh ginger, grated
1	tablespoon cumin seeds
2	teaspoons salt
1	tablespoon garam masala
1	tablespoon turmeric
1/4	teaspoon red chili powder
1	tablespoon mango powder
1	cup chopped tomatoes (canned is ideal for this)
2	pounds potatoes (approximately), peeled and cut into 1 1/2″ cubes (see "Notes")
3	cups boiling water
3	tablespoons dried fenugreek leaves
1	cup plain yogurt—I use whole-milk in this recipe (optional)
	a handful of cilantro, chopped—to garnish

- Heat the oil for a minute or so over a medium heat in a deep saucepan.

- Add the onions, ginger, and cumin seeds, stir, and cook until soft and the onions are translucent—this will take about 5 minutes.

- Stir in the salt, garam masala, turmeric, chili powder, and mango powder. Cook the spices for 2 minutes—do not allow to burn.

- Put in the tomatoes. Stir well and cook the ingredients over a low/medium flame for 5 minutes to allow a thick paste to develop.

- Add the potatoes, coat well with the tomato mixture, and cover the pan for 5 minutes.

- Add 3 cups of boiling water and the fenugreek leaves. Bring the contents of the pan to a boil for 1 minute, turn the heat down to medium, cover, and simmer for 20 minutes until the potatoes are cooked through. Add a little more water here if you prefer more "sauce."

- Five minutes before serving, you may turn the heat down and fold in a cup of yogurt (optional). This just brings a level of creaminess to the dish (test for salt as adding yogurt sometimes calls for an adjustment). Heat through.

- Garnish with cilantro.

Done.

ALLOO, SUKHE (DRY, SPICED POTATOES)

A victorious option for the vegetarian...

Serves: 6
Preparation time: 10 minutes
Cooking time: 35–40 minutes
Notes: I use white or yukon gold potatoes—I am not really fussy.
Begin with the potatoes (approximately 2 pounds). Put into a large pan with enough water to cover the potatoes. Bring the water to a boil, cover the pot with a tight-fitting lid, turn the heat to low/medium, and allow to simmer for about 55–60 minutes until the potatoes are cooked through. A knife should easily slide through the middle of the potato. Check that there is enough water to cover the potatoes as they cook and add more if need be. Remove from the heat. Drain in a colander until cool. The peel should scrape off easily—discard. Roughly chop the potatoes into 1 1/2"–2" chunks.
Serving suggestion: Serve in toasted bread buns.
M/A: Yes. Just heat before serving.
* No

4	tablespoons canola oil
1	medium onion, finely sliced
1	tablespoon fresh ginger, grated
1	tablespoon cumin seeds
2	teaspoons salt
1	tablespoon garam masala
1	tablespoon turmeric
1/4	teaspoon red chili powder
1	tablespoon mango powder
1	cup chopped tomatoes (canned is ideal for this)
2	pounds potatoes (approximately), peeled, boiled, and roughly chopped (see "Notes")
1	cup boiling water (approximately)
1	cup plain yogurt—I use whole-milk in this recipe (optional)
	a handful of cilantro, chopped—to garnish

- Heat the oil for a minute or so over medium heat in a wide, shallow pan.

- Add the onions, ginger, and cumin seeds, stir, and cook until soft and the onions are translucent—this will take about 5 minutes.

- Stir in the salt, garam masala, turmeric, chili powder, and mango powder. Cook the spices for 2 minutes—do not allow to burn.

- Put in the tomatoes. Stir well and cook the ingredients over a low/medium flame for 5 minutes to allow a thick paste to develop.

- Add the potatoes, coat well with the tomato mixture (add a cup of boiling water at this point if it will help to coat the potatoes with the tomato mixture), and cover the pan for 5 minutes. Heat through and stir to prevent burning.

- Five minutes before serving, you might fold in a cup of yogurt (optional). This just brings a level of creaminess to the dish (test for salt as adding yogurt sometimes calls for an adjustment). Heat through.

- Garnish with cilantro.

Done.

BHINDI (LADIES' FINGERS/OKRA)

Bhindi often appears at my mum's table because both my dad and sister jump at it. I have learned to appreciate this quite flavorful dish now that I cook it for my own children. The initial draw for my poppets was the horror and giggles that came with gobbling down "ladies' fingers"!

Serves: 4 as a side dish
Preparation time: 15 minutes
Cooking time: 30 minutes
Notes: When buying your okra, the body of the vegetable should be firm and the end tip should snap off easily to ensure maximum freshness—check this before you buy. Take care—if the vegetable is not dried well, it may create a slimy texture in the finished dish. Slice the top and the bottom from the okra and then chop to the desired size.
Serving suggestion: With chapattis (see "Breads" section).
M/A: Yes. Just heat before serving.
* No

3	tablespoons canola oil
1	small onion, finely sliced
1	tablespoon cumin seeds
1	teaspoon salt
1	tablespoon garam masala
1	teaspoon turmeric
1/2	teaspoon red chili powder
1	teaspoon mango powder
1	pound okra/ladies' fingers, washed, dried, chopped into 1" pieces (see "Notes")

- Heat the oil over a medium flame for a minute or so. Add the onion and cumin seeds, turn the heat up to medium/high, and stir for 5 minutes or so.

- Add the salt, garam masala, turmeric, chili powder, and mango powder. Cook the spices for a further 2 minutes—do not allow to burn.

- Fold in the okra, coat well with the spiced onions, and cook for 5 minutes. Stir occasionally.

- Cover the pan, turn the heat to low/medium, and cook for 15 minutes. Stir once or twice during this time.

Done.

BAINGAN (EGGPLANT/AUBERGINE)

The flesh of the eggplant is able to absorb large amounts of fat, sauces, and hence flavor. The resulting dish is often quite rich and substantial—therefore a perfect inclusion in any vegetarian meal. It is no wonder then, that this versatile fruit is so apparent in many world cuisines. Each mouthful of this preparation will unearth an explosion of flavors.

Serves: 4–6 as a side dish
Preparation time: 10–15 minutes
Cooking time: 45 minutes
Serving suggestion: Alongside your favorite crackers or bread. Hummus is a super accompaniment too.
M/A: Yes. It tastes better the next day. Just heat before serving.
* Yes. I have frozen leftovers of this dish before.

3	tablespoons canola oil
1	medium onion, sliced
1	tablespoon fresh ginger, grated
1	tablespoon cumin seeds
1 1/2	teaspoons salt
1	tablespoon garam masala
1	tablespoon turmeric
1/4	teaspoon red chili powder
2	teaspoons mango powder
1	cup chopped/crushed tomatoes (canned is ideal here)
1	large eggplant (approximately 1–1 1/2 pounds), chopped into 1″ cubes
1	cup water (may be needed)
	a handful of cilantro, chopped—to garnish

- Heat the oil over a medium heat in a non-stick, deep saucepan.

- Add the onions, ginger, and cumin seeds, stir, and cook until soft and the onions are translucent—this will take about 5 minutes.

- Stir in the salt, garam masala, turmeric, chili powder, and mango powder. Cook the spices for 2 minutes—do not allow to burn.

- Put in the tomatoes. Stir well and cook the ingredients over a low/medium flame for 5 minutes to allow a thick paste to develop.

- Turn the heat to medium and throw in the eggplant. Coat well with the paste, cover, and cook for 30 minutes until the eggplant is cooked. (Mix contents of the pan every 5 minutes or so to prevent sticking—if it all appears too dry, mix in 1/2 cup of water at a time as you go along and reduce the flame if need be.)

- After 30 minutes, stir and switch off the heat. Leave the pan covered for a further 10 minutes.

Done.

BAINGAN KA BHARTHA
(MASHED EGGPLANT/AUBERGINE)

Something similar to a "baba ganoush"...smooth, smoky, and simply superb.

Serves: 6 as a side dish
Preparation time: 1 hour or so (includes **Step 1**—see recipe below)
Cooking time: 30 minutes
Notes: Take a moment to read through this recipe so that you are prepared for **Step 1**.
You can make a "bharta" using many vegetables, however, eggplant is the most popular in Punjabi cuisine.
Serving suggestion: As a toast topping with hummus and crispy onions.
M/A: Yes. It is even better the following day.
* Yes

Step 1:

1	very large or 2 medium eggplants (total of approximately 1 1/2 –2 pounds)
1	tablespoon (approximately) canola oil

Step 2:

4	tablespoons canola oil
1	tablespoon cumin seeds
1	medium onion, finely sliced
2"	piece of fresh ginger, peeled and cut into juliennes
1	teaspoon salt
2	teaspoons garam masala
1/2	teaspoon red chili powder
2	dried bay leaves
3/4	cup chopped tomatoes (canned is ideal for this) or 2 large tomatoes, diced
	prepared eggplant (see "Step 1" in recipe below)
1	cup frozen peas
	a handful of cilantro, chopped—to garnish

Step 1:

- Wash and thoroughly dry the eggplant.

- Using your hands, smear the skin with a tablespoon of canola oil and place on a foil-lined baking tray. Prick all sides using a fork and then pop the tray under a pre-heated broiler (medium/high heat).

- Allow the eggplant to cook and be sure to turn every 10 minutes until the skin is charred on all areas—this will take about 50 minutes.

- Remove from the heat and let the eggplant cool for 20 minutes.

- Now, using your fingers and holding the "crown" of the eggplant, peel away and discard the blistered skin.

- Take a clean plate and still holding the top of the vegetable, use a fork to mash away the flesh—this is your treasure.

- Put aside or refrigerate until you are ready for **Step 2**.

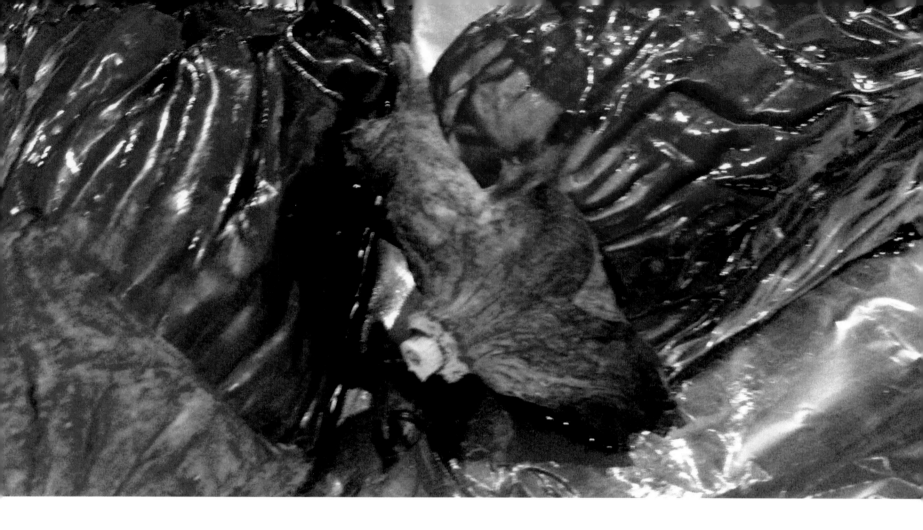

Step 2:

- Over medium heat, warm the oil in a frying pan.

- Add the cumin seeds, onion, and ginger—turn the heat to medium/high and cook the ingredients for 8–10 minutes. Stir regularly to prevent sticking.

- Mix in the salt, garam masala, chili powder, and bay leaves. Bring the heat down to medium and cook for a minute or so.

- Put the tomatoes in at this point, stir well, and cook for 5 minutes—do not allow the mix to burn so keep **stirring**.

- Turn the heat up to medium/high and add the (prepared) eggplant. Allow the flavors to marry; keep stirring for about 5 minutes.

- Pour in the peas and continue to cook for a further 5 minutes.

- Turn the heat to low and cover for the final 2–3 minutes.

- Garnish with cilantro.

- **Done.**

This fabulous pizza is reason enough to buy an eggplant. Top a **ready-made pizza base** with the **baingan** (from either of the previous two recipes). Heat in the oven and garnish liberally with **feta cheese**, **chopped red onions**, and **cilantro**.

Elevate a simple bite—try either of the **baingan** recipes as a topping for **mini bread rounds** and **hummus** and finish with **cilantro** and **fried onions**.

THORI (ZUCCHINI/COURGETTE)

This is one of the first Indian vegetable recipes that I introduced my children to. It is soft, squidgy, and envelops all of the flavors that I wanted them to become accustomed to. In the beginning I would omit the chili powder and ginger, but now that their tastes have evolved, I make the real deal and serve alongside a bread and plain yogurt.

Serves: 4 as a side dish
Preparation time: 10 minutes
Cooking time: 35 minutes
Serving suggestion: With chapattis (see "Breads" section).
M/A: Yes. Just heat before serving.
* No. It tends to become a little "watery."

3	tablespoons canola oil
1	onion, finely chopped
1	tablespoon fresh ginger, grated
1	tablespoon cumin seeds
1 1/2	teaspoons salt
1	teaspoon garam masala
1	teaspoon turmeric
1/4	teaspoon red chili powder
2	medium tomatoes, chopped **OR** 1 cup chopped/crushed tomatoes (canned is ideal here) zucchini, chopped into 1/2" pieces (approximately 1 1/2 pounds or 4 medium-sized zucchini)

- Heat the oil over low/medium heat in a large, non-stick frying pan for a minute or so.

- Add the onions, ginger, and cumin seeds, stir, and cook until soft and the onions are translucent—this will take about 5 minutes.

- Stir in the salt, garam masala, turmeric, and chili powder. Cook the spices for 2 minutes—do not allow to burn.

- Put in the tomatoes. Stir well and cook the ingredients for 5 minutes which will allow a thick paste to evolve.

- Add the zucchini, coat well with the cooked ingredients, cover the pan, mix at intervals, and cook for approximately 20 minutes.

Done.

LENTILS, BEANS, AND PULSES...
I do not comprehend the differences, so we will just agree to refer to all as "dal."

Moong/mung dal (yellow, split lentils from the whole moong/mung bean)—as a soup	66
Moong/mung dal, sukhi (yellow, split lentils from the whole moong/mung bean)—dry	68
Rajma (kidney beans)	70
Rongi (black-eyed peas)	72
Chana, sukhe (dry garbanzo beans/chickpeas)	74
Chana masala/Chole (garbanzo bean/chickpea curry)	76
Dal makhani (urad lentils—buttery)	78
Moong/mung bean salad (whole moong/mung bean salad)	82

MOONG/MUNG DAL (YELLOW, SPLIT LENTILS)—as a soup

The simplest of all lentils to make. It requires the minimum of ingredients and because of that reason alone is often referred to as a "poor man's food." There is a valid reason, however, that this is my dad's, husband's, and son's most requested accompaniment to rice—it provides delicious simplicity with every slurp. I introduced my children to this dal before any other as it is easy to digest, and I could be sure they were getting a protein-packed meal from the get-go. "Yellow" dal, as we call it, is true comfort food—it tastes like "home."

Serves: 8–12
Preparation time: 10 minutes
Cooking time: 1 hour
Notes: Be certain to buy the "split" moong bean (yellow) as opposed to the "whole" moong bean (green).
You will need a really deep soup pan to hold the yield of this recipe—my pan is an 8-quart stockpot.
The "tadka" (dressing)—though flavorful—is not essential. One might eat the lentils as a simple soup; plop in a knob of salted butter—yum!
I sometimes throw in a bag of spinach and a couple of sliced tomatoes at the beginning of making this dish—depending upon what I want the children to consume or, quite honestly, what can be found in my fridge that day.
Look at "Breads" section for an idea on how to use leftover dal—dal parantha.
Serving suggestion: As a soup, with chapattis (see "Breads" section), or over mattar pulau (see "Rice" section).
M/A: Yes. Just heat before serving.
* Yes

2	cups split moong dal (split moong/mung beans)
12	cups cold water (and maybe some more)
1	medium onion, finely sliced
2	tablespoons fresh ginger, grated
1	tablespoon salted butter
1	tablespoon salt
1	tablespoon turmeric

"tadka": (see "Notes")

2	tablespoons canola oil
1	tablespoon salted butter
1	medium onion, finely sliced
2	tablespoons cumin seeds
$1/2$	teaspoon salt
$1 1/2$	tablespoons garam masala
$1/2$	teaspoon red chili powder (optional)

a handful of cilantro, chopped—to garnish

- Use a really deep pan to wash the moong dal vigorously under running water. Use your hand to loosen any dirt particles on the lentils. Discard the dirty water and add 12 cups of cold water, the onion, ginger, butter, salt, and turmeric to the clean dal.

- Bring the contents of the pan to a boil, then cover with a lid and turn the heat to medium—take care it does not boil over; adjust the heat as needed.

- Allow to cook for 1 hour. I like my dal thick, so I add little additional water but take the time to occasionally peer inside, stir very gently, and add 2 or 3 more cups of water if you wish for a looser consistency.

- Meanwhile, in a frying pan you can begin the tadka (the spiced dressing of the dish). Melt the butter with the oil over medium heat for a minute or so.

- Add the onion and the cumin seeds, mix, and cook for 10 minutes or so until the onions are browning—do not allow to burn. Sprinkle in the salt, garam masala, and red chili powder and cook for a further 2 minutes. You can save the tadka to dress the whole dish (make sure it is hot) before serving, or you can mix into the lentils while they cook—the choice is yours.

- Garnish with cilantro.

Done.

MOONG/MUNG DAL, SUKHI (YELLOW, SPLIT LENTILS)— dry

Just a different way to present moong dal. The combination of firm lentils, caramelized onions, cumin, ginger, cilantro, and lemon affords each spoonful with a freshness, fragrance, and nuttiness that you will want to visit again and again.

Serves: 6 as a side dish
Preparation time: 10 minutes
Cooking time: 25–30 minutes (can be less if you are able to cook dal and "tadka" simultaneously)
Notes: Be certain to buy the "split" moong bean (yellow) as opposed to the "whole" moong bean (green).
If you crave extra onions on your hot dog, you may want to double the amount of fried ones for your "tadka" (dressing).
Serving suggestion: With chapattis (see "Breads" section) and raita (see "Accompaniments" section).
M/A: Yes. Just heat before serving.
* No

2	cups split moong dal (split moong/mung beans)
8	cups cold water
1	tablespoon salt
2	teaspoons turmeric

"tadka": (see "Notes")

4	tablespoons canola oil
2	tablespoons cumin seeds
1	medium onion, finely sliced
1	tablespoon fresh ginger, grated
1/2	teaspoon salt
2	teaspoons garam masala
1/4–1/2	teaspoon red chili powder
1	teaspoon packed brown sugar

a handful of cilantro, chopped—to garnish
juice of 1 lemon—to dress, double if you prefer tangy

- Use a deep soup pan to wash the moong dal vigorously under running water. Use your hand to loosen any dirt particles on the lentils. Discard the dirty water and add 8 cups of cold water, the salt, and the turmeric to the clean dal.

- Bring the contents of the pan to a boil and, as soon as it does, turn the heat to medium/high (taking care to monitor so the water does not boil over). Stir once to check that the lentils have not clumped together and allow to bubble for 8 minutes exactly—no longer; be vigilant not to overcook. Use a timer and taste a lentil—it should be "al dente." Using a sieve, drain immediately. Put aside.

- Now prepare the tadka (dressing for the lentils). Heat the oil in a frying pan over medium heat for a minute or so. Add the cumin seeds, onion, and ginger, stir regularly, turn the heat to medium/high, and cook for 10–12 minutes.

- Sprinkle in the spices and sugar, turn the heat down to medium, and cook for a further 5 minutes. I allow my onions to caramelize (or burn slightly)—how much is your choice.

- Dress the top of the warm lentils before serving or toss the tadka with the warm lentils, cilantro, and lemon juice to really blend all the flavors—best when stirred in the tadka pan itself.

Done.

RAJMA (KIDNEY BEANS)

Rich, filling, robust, and a hearty, vegetarian chili are the best descriptions for this inviting plate. Start with dried kidney beans and not the canned variety as it is the long cooking process that yields such a bold and flavorful result. Alongside rice and a red onion salad (see "Accompaniments" section), rajma serves as a complete and wholesome meal. I have friends who use a pressure cooker to prepare their pulses, but to be honest, they scare me to death (the cookers). These beans are so scrumptious that they are worth a little planning.

Serves: 8
Preparation time: Overnight soaking + Masala 1 (p. xxxviii)
Cooking time: 3 hours
Notes: Soak the beans in lots of cold water (the volume of water should be at least 4″ above the beans as they will swell). Leave for about 10 hours...not much longer. I soak overnight and cook in the morning.
You will prepare Masala 1 recipe—only half of the Masala 1 is needed for this rajma recipe so just freeze the remainder for another time.
I occasionally add a hefty knob of salted butter for a richer and silkier sauce.
Serving suggestion: Over white rice (see "Rice" section).
M/A: Yes. Just heat before serving.
* Yes

4	cups red kidney beans, uncooked (see "Notes")
1/2	part of Masala 1 (p. xxxviii)
2 1/2–3	pints boiling water
2	tablespoons dried fenugreek leaves
	salt to taste
	a handful of cilantro, chopped—to garnish

- Rinse and drain the pre-soaked kidney beans (see "Notes").

- Heat the already prepared Masala 1 (just half of the portion) in a deep pan.

- Add the kidney beans, stir, and coat well with the Masala 1.

- Pour in 2 1/2 pints of boiling water (enough so that the beans are immersed in water) and add the dried fenugreek leaves.

- Bring the pot to a boil over high heat, place on a tight-fitting lid, turn the heat to low/medium, and allow the rajma to simmer for about 3 hours. During cooking, check that the liquid level remains at least 2″ above the beans—add boiling water if need be. Stir gently, perhaps every 30 minutes, to ensure that the beans are not sticking to the base of the pan—lower the heat slightly if you need to.

- Taste a bean—it should be soft and demand no effort to bite into, and then taste a spoonful of the liquid to check for salt and add 1 teaspoon or so if needed—it usually is required.

Done.

RONGI (BLACK-EYED PEAS)

Living in the South, custom speaks of the prosperity that eating black-eyed peas brings at New Year. The traditional Georgia version is boiled with salt. I choose to serve it my own way every December 31. My Atlantan friends do not complain—I imagine good luck is good luck no matter which recipe beckons it.

Serves: 8
Preparation time: Overnight soaking + Masala 1 (p. xxxviii)
Cooking time: 1 hour
Notes: Soak the beans in lots of cold water (the volume of water should be at least 4″ above the beans as they will swell). Leave for about 10 hours...not much longer. I soak overnight and cook in the morning.
You will prepare Masala 1 recipe—only half of the Masala 1 is needed for this rongi recipe so just freeze the remainder for another time.
I occasionally add a hefty knob of salted butter for a richer and silkier sauce.
Serving suggestion: Over white rice (see "Rice" section).
M/A: Yes. Just heat before serving.
* Yes

4	cups black-eyed peas, uncooked (see "Notes")
1/2	part of Masala 1 (p. xxxviii)
2 1/2−3	pints boiling water
2	tablespoons dried fenugreek leaves
	salt to taste
	a handful of cilantro, chopped—to garnish

- Rinse and drain the pre-soaked black-eyed peas (see "Notes").

- Heat the already prepared Masala 1 (just half of the portion) in a deep pan.

- Add the black-eyed peas, stir, and coat well with the Masala 1.

- Pour in 2 1/2 pints of boiling water (enough so that the beans are immersed in water) and add the dried fenugreek leaves.

- Bring the pot to a boil over a high heat, place on a tight-fitting lid, turn the heat to low/medium, and allow the rongi to simmer for about 45–60 minutes. During cooking, check that the liquid level remains at least 2″ above the beans—add boiling water if need be. Stir gently, perhaps every 20 minutes, to ensure that the beans are not sticking to the base of the pan—lower the heat slightly if you need to.

- Taste a bean—it should be soft and demand no effort to bite into, and then taste a spoonful of the liquid to check for salt and add 1 teaspoon or so if needed—it usually is required.

Done.

CHANA, SUKHE (DRY GARBANZO BEANS/CHICKPEAS)

One of our dearest friends would kill for these chickpeas. We sometimes play impromptu, friendly poker in our neighborhood, and because they are so quick to make (and all of the ingredients are already in my pantry), I often serve these before the game. Our guest is more than content with a generous helping of sukhe chana, naan bread (store-bought), and cucumber raita (see "Accompaniments" section)—he does not even notice when some of his chips go walking. The laugh is on us though; he wipes his plate and the table clean—every time! These garbanzo beans can also be served at room temperature, so they were always my mum's choice when going on a "family" picnic. I smile because it was NEVER the four of us...always at least eight "aunties," eight "uncles," a few grandparents, and dozens of children. I recall the joy that chaos, a soccer ball, and sharing bread and beans can bring.

Serves: 8 as a side dish
Preparation time: 2 minutes
Cooking time: 15 minutes
Notes: I use canned garbanzo beans as I find they hold their shape well while being seasoned and stirred.
Serving suggestion: Serve with pooris (see "Breads" section) or store-bought naan bread.
This dish is also great when eaten at room temperature.
M/A: Yes. Eat at room temperature or just heat before serving.
* No

4	tablespoons canola oil
2	tablespoons cumin seeds
1	teaspoon salt
2	tablespoons garam masala
1/2	teaspoon red chili powder
2	tablespoons pomegranate powder
4	cans ready-cooked garbanzo beans— approximately 15 ounces, rinsed and drained
1/2	small red onion, chopped—to garnish
	a handful of cilantro, chopped—to garnish
	juice of a lemon—to dress

- Heat the oil in a frying pan over medium/high heat for 1 minute.

- Add the cumin seeds and cook for 1 minute.

- Now put in the salt, garam masala, red chili powder, and pomegranate powder. Stir well for 2–3 minutes—do not allow to burn. The release of aromas is something fabulous.

- Add the garbanzo beans, coat well with the oil and the spices, and regularly stir for 5 minutes over medium heat.

- Cover the pan. Allow the beans to cook for a further 5 minutes. Stir once or twice to be sure that the beans are not burning.

- Remove from the heat, garnish with the onions, cilantro, and lemon juice.

Done.

CHANA MASALA/CHOLE (GARBANZO BEAN/CHICKPEA CURRY)

Almost always paired with bhatura (see "Breads" section), our family also enjoys chana masala with potato-filled samosas at "Diwali." This is one of the biggest and most-celebrated Hindu festivals. It is also known as the "Festival of Lights" and marks the Hindu New Year (based on the lunar calendar). People's homes are lit with candles, the skies are a show of fireworks, most try to clear their debts and clean their home from top to bottom. The hope is that "Laxmi" (the goddess of wealth) will visit with the good fortune of cash or toys in the New Year (my children's bedrooms are never so tidy). It is an immensely joyous time where families and friends gather to eat, drink, exchange gifts, play cards, and above all, be merry. "Happy Diwali!"

Serves: 8
Preparation time: 10 minutes
Cooking time: 30–35 minutes
Notes: I use canned garbanzo beans as I find they hold their shape while being seasoned and stirred.
I am loosely referring to this dish as a "curry," indicating the Western notion of a deeply flavored "saucy" dish. You will notice that no curry powder (a commercially prepared mixture of spices) is used as most Indian homes do not utilize this ingredient.
Serving suggestion: With white rice (see "Rice" section), raita (see "Accompaniments" section), or your favorite bread (try bhatura in the "Breads" section—it is the most popular choice).
M/A: Yes. Just heat before serving.
* No

4	tablespoons canola oil
1	large onion, finely chopped
2	tablespoons fresh ginger, finely grated
1 ½	tablespoons cumin seeds
2 ½	teaspoons salt
2	tablespoons garam masala
1	teaspoon turmeric
1	teaspoon red chili powder
1 ½	tablespoons mango powder
1	cup chopped/crushed tomatoes (canned is ideal here)
2"–3"	cinnamon stick (optional)
4	cans ready-cooked garbanzo beans— approximately 15 ounces, rinsed and drained
2 ½–3	cups boiling water (depends upon required consistency)
	a handful of cilantro, chopped—to garnish
2	jalapeno peppers or serrano chilis, sliced—to garnish (optional)

- Heat the oil for 1 minute over a medium flame and add the onions, ginger, and cumin seeds. Cook for 8–10 minutes until the onions have softened. Mix occasionally during this time to prevent sticking.

- Season with the salt, garam masala, turmeric, red chili powder, and mango powder. Cook for 2–3 minutes—do not allow to burn.

- Add the tomatoes (and cinnamon—optional), stir, and cook for a further 4–5 minutes. A thick tomato paste will develop.

- Mix in the garbanzo beans, coat with the tomato mixture, add the boiling water, bring to a boil over high heat, and gently stir once more.

- Place on the lid and turn the heat to low/medium. Allow the contents to simmer for 12–15 minutes.

- Garnish with the jalapeno peppers or serrano chilis and cilantro.

Done.

DAL MAKHANI (URAD LENTILS—BUTTERY)

Although eaten on any occasion, the mere mention transports me to "Karvachauth." This is a custom where Hindu married women fast all day—it is quite strict as not even water is to be drank. In our home, the lentils simmer for much of the day in anticipation of the evening meal. Wives hope for the good health, long life, prosperity, and overall well-being of their spouse. They also pray for the moon to rise early that night as it is at its appearance that food may be taken. It is such a festive time amongst Punjabi ladies—they visit the beauty parlor, adorn themselves in bridal colors (red, pink, orange), have henna patterns applied to their hands, and do their best to be patient and never outwardly complain of hunger! While viewing and worshipping the moon, the (starving but doting) wife asks her (appreciative) husband if she may break her fast. Sanjay usually pauses, smiles, laughs aloud, and the feast begins. (I know you are wondering about the "husband's fast"—well, mmm, it does not exist.)

Serves: A whole party, 14–18 at least
Preparation time: Overnight soaking + 10 minutes
Cooking time: 5 hours
Notes: Soak the lentils and beans together in lots of cold water (the volume of water should be at least 4″ above the lentils and beans as they will swell). Leave for about 10 hours...not much longer. I soak overnight and cook in the morning.

You will need a really deep soup pan to hold the yield of this recipe (my pan is an 8-quart stockpot) and have your kettle boiling too—you will require lots of boiling water for this dal.

You will not overcook this dal. If you leave it bubbling for an extra half an hour, there is no harm done.

Once cooked, you can fish out the cloves, cinnamon, and cardamom if you like, or do what I do...warn my friends to put aside if they come across one in their bowl.

This dish takes such a long time to cook that it makes sense to make the large amount that I have suggested and then freeze half of it in your required portion sizes.

You may also know this dal as "kali" (or "black") dal.
Serving suggestion: Over white rice (see "Rice" section) or with parantha (see "Breads" section).
M/A: Yes. It is fabulous the following day.
* Yes—that is precisely why I make such a large amount.

3 ½	cups mapte/black ("urad") lentils (see "Notes")
1 ½	cups kidney beans (see "Notes")
6	pints boiling water—you will need more as you move through
1	large onion, sliced
4	cloves
3″	cinnamon stick
1	black cardamom (cracked open)
3	tablespoons fresh ginger, grated
2	tablespoons salted butter
1	tablespoon salt (a little extra too—if needed)
1–1 ½	cups heavy/double/whipping cream (if you do not have it, milk will work)

"tadka":

2	tablespoons salted butter
3	tablespoons canola oil
1	medium onion, finely sliced
2	tablespoons cumin seeds
½	teaspoon salt
2	tablespoons garam masala
1	teaspoon red chili powder (optional)
	a handful of cilantro, chopped—to garnish

● Rinse and drain the lentils and beans (see "Notes") and put into the deepest pot you have. Follow with the boiling water, onion, cloves, cinnamon, cardamom pod, ginger, butter, and salt.

● Bring to a boil over a high flame, stir gently, cover, turn heat to medium, and simmer for about 5 hours. (Yes!)

(continued...)

- While all is cooking, check to see that the liquid level is at least 3″ above the lentils and beans—add 3–4 cups of boiling water at a time as needed. Stir gently, perhaps every 30 minutes, to ensure that the contents are not sticking to the base of the pan—if they are sticking, turn the flame to low. The dal will begin to take on a creamy appearance.

- After about 4 ½ hours, prepare the tadka (dressing for the dish). In a separate frying pan, heat the butter and the oil over a medium flame for 1 minute. Add the cumin seeds and onion and cook for 8–10 minutes or so. Stir to avoid any burning. Sprinkle in the salt, garam masala, and red chili powder (optional) and cook the seasonings for a further 2–3 minutes. Add the tadka to the large pot, stir, and simmer for a further 10 minutes or so.

- Now that the lentils and the beans are cooked, pour in the cream and heat through for 5–10 minutes, then taste the dal for salt and add 1 teaspoon or so if needed—it is usually required.

- Garnish with cilantro.

Done.

MOONG/MUNG BEAN SALAD (WHOLE MOONG/MUNG BEAN SALAD)

Colorful, refreshing, inviting, and good for you? Get soaking and I am sure you will agree.

Serves: 12–14 as a side salad
Preparation time: 5 minutes washing + 3 days waiting + 15 minutes for chopping and dressing
Cooking time: N/A
Notes: Do not confuse this bean with the yellow lentil ("split" moong/mung bean)—it will not work with that one! This recipe calls for the "whole" moong bean (green). Organize yourself and do what I do—make a note on your calendar so you do not forget about the beans.
Serving suggestion: Serve as a salad and alongside your meats or vegetables at a lunch or dinner. Feel free to add celery, chopped apples, raisins, nuts, etc.—you should make this salad your own.
M/A: No
***** No

2	cups whole moong dal (see "Notes")
	lots of cold water for soaking

dressing:

	juice of 2–3 lemons
1–1 1/2	tablespoons salt
1 1/2	teaspoons black pepper
1	tablespoon mango powder
2	tomatoes, chopped
1/2	medium red onion, chopped
1	English cucumber, chopped
1	red bell pepper, chopped
	a huge handful of cilantro, chopped

- **Day 1, p.m.**—wash 3 cups of whole moong dal vigorously under running water. Use your hand to loosen any dirt particles on the lentils. Discard the dirty water. Soak the beans in a bowlful of cold water overnight—12 hours at least. The volume of water should be at least 3″ above the beans as the beans may swell.

- **Day 2, a.m.**—rinse the beans and replenish the bowl with fresh water.

- **Day 2, p.m.**—rinse the beans again and replenish the bowl with fresh water.

- **Day 3, a.m.**—take a kitchen towel (large enough to hold and wrap the beans) and rinse in cold tap water. Now, squeeze it out. Rinse the beans once more and drain them into a colander lined with the wet kitchen hand towel. You will notice that they have swelled slightly. Tightly wrap the beans and tie the wet towel using an elastic band. Put the "package" into a clean bowl, cover with a fresh towel, and place in a dark place for 24–36 hours. (Pantry perhaps?)

- **Day 4, a.m. or p.m.**—you may unwrap the sprouted beans. Put the beans into a clean bowl, wash thoroughly under cold running water (peel off any that may have stuck to the towel), and drain well in a colander. Refrigerate until ready to dress—that same day is optimum as the beans will begin to dry out by Day 5.

- **To serve:** toss with a liberal amount of lemon juice, salt, black pepper, mango powder, chopped tomatoes, chopped red onion, chopped cucumber, chopped bell pepper, chopped cilantro (I am offering estimations here—it is your salad, design it as you wish). Chill.

Done.

POULTRY, MEAT, AND FISH...

TANDOORI CHICKEN/CHICKEN TIKKA

You have just turned to both a healthy and appetizing recipe for preparing your protein. "Tandoori" indicates that the ingredient is cooked in a "tandoor" (an extremely hot clay oven)—most Indian homes, including my own, do not own one so most resort to using their conventional oven. "Tikka" means "chunks" or "pieces" and includes the traditional tandoori chicken, lamb, shrimp, or paneer (cheese) that is found on many North Indian restaurant menus. The dish usually arrives in a brilliant red version of what I am offering here, but there is no need for crimson food coloring, in my opinion. The real requirement is clean fingers and your most favored beer.

Serves: 10–12 as a light bite
Preparation time: 10 minutes + marinating time (4–5 hours)
Cooking time: 20–25 minutes
Notes: Equally easy to thread onto skewers for the grill. Super when eaten alone or use to build a sandwich.
Serving suggestion: With a raita and kachumbar salad (see "Accompaniments" section).
M/A: Yes. Just heat before serving.
* Yes. I often marinate my chicken and then freeze. When I need it, I thaw, pour off any "watery" liquid that may be present, and bake as below.

1 ¾	cups plain yogurt—I use whole-milk or low-fat but not fat-free
1	tablespoon canola oil
1 ½	teaspoons salt
1 ½	tablespoons garam masala
1 ½	teaspoons red chili powder
1 ½	tablespoons mango powder
1 ½	tablespoons pomegranate powder
3	tablespoons dried fenugreek leaves
1	teaspoon ginger powder
1	teaspoon chopped garlic (optional)
3 ½–4	pounds chicken breasts, diced into 1 ½" pieces a handful of cilantro, chopped—to garnish juice of a lemon—to dress

- Combine all of the ingredients except for the chicken, cilantro, and lemon juice in a mixing bowl. This is your marinade.

- Put in the chicken. Stir well.

- Cover and refrigerate for at least 4–5 hours—overnight would be perfect. The yogurt will tenderize the chicken.

- Spread onto a foil-lined baking tray and bake in the middle of the oven (375°F) for about 20–25 minutes. Mix once or twice during this time. (You might notice the juices running off; if so, pull out the tray and drain off as much of the liquid as you are able to.) Back into the oven.

- Check that the chicken is cooked (cut through a piece…it should show no pink). Discard any extra juices left on the tray.

- Squeeze the fresh lemon juice over the chicken and garnish with cilantro.

Done.

TANDOORI SHRIMP

Use the same marinade (as that of tandoori chicken—on the previous page) to coat the raw shrimp and then refrigerate for up to 2 hours. Thread onto pre-soaked wooden skewers and grill. I like to eat them with a mango and cilantro raita (see "Accompaniments" section).

TANDOORI LAMB

Again, marinate the lamb (use the marinade recipe from the previous page), refrigerate for at least 6 hours (overnight is great) and throw onto the grill or pop in the oven. If using boneless lamb pieces, try it in a sandwich with alloo, sukhe (see "Vegetables" section). Quite fabulous.

CHICKEN TIKKA MASALA

It is believed that this popular Indian dish originated in Britain. Was it in Glasgow or a London curry house? One could argue forever. There is no need to cross the Atlantic...you can relish this at your very own table. Oh and forget cucumber sandwiches and scones...this recipe so transports me back to England that I made it to celebrate Queen Elizabeth's recent Jubilee!

Serves: 8–10 as a main dish
Preparation time: 5 minutes + preparation of chicken tikka recipe (p. 86)
Cooking time: 20 minutes
Notes: Only add 1 cup of cream if you prefer a hotter version of this recipe.
Serving suggestion: Over white rice (see "Rice" section).
M/A: Yes. Just add the chicken and heat before serving.
* Yes

For the sauce: heat **2 tablespoons canola oil** and **2 tablespoons salted butter** over medium heat; add **1 tablespoon cumin seeds** and **a medium onion (thinly sliced)**. Cook for 5–7 minutes until the onions appear translucent. Add **1 teaspoon salt, 1 tablespoon garam masala, 1 teaspoon red chili powder, 2 tablespoons tomato paste/puree** and cook for 2–3 minutes—do not allow to burn. Mix in **1 ½ cups chopped/crushed tomatoes** and simmer over a low flame for 5 minutes. Pour in **1 ½ cups of heavy cream** and gently warm through for 2–3 minutes.

Add the chicken just before serving and allow to heat through; garnish with **cilantro**.

Done.

CHICKEN MAKHANI (BUTTER CHICKEN)

Frankly, to indulge in this delight is nothing short of spoiling yourself rotten. Salted butter, heavy cream, ground nuts (mmm...my children refer to the dish as "chicken nuttini")—I promise myself that the extra boot-camp session is well worth it. (Actually, I have repeatedly and unsuccessfully endeavored to invite the trainer over for dinner—I would like to say it is her loss, but in fact it is food-lovers, like myself, who keep my dear friend in business! My gain is her gain...)

Serves: 8
Preparation time: 10 minutes + preparation of Masala 2 (p. xl)
Cooking time: 25 minutes
Notes: If you have any extra Weight Watchers points to spare (how?) you might garnish the finished dish with crushed, unsalted pistachio nuts (approximately ¹/₂ cup).
Serving suggestion: With white rice (see "Rice" section) or with dressed up pita (see "Breads" section).
M/A: Yes. Just heat before serving.
* Yes

2	tablespoons salted butter
1	portion of prepared Masala 2 (p. xl)
2	pounds chicken breasts (approximately), diced into 1 ¹/₂" pieces
1	cup unsalted almonds, ground
2	cups heavy/double/whipping cream

- Melt the butter over medium heat in a large shallow frying pan.

- Add Masala 2 and heat through for 4–5 minutes.

- Stir in the chicken, coat with the Masala 2, and allow to cook. This will take 8–10 minutes. Mix at intervals to prevent sticking.

- Spoon in the almonds and combine well for a further minute.

- Pour in the cream, turn the heat to low, cover with a lid, and allow all the flavors to blend and heat through. This will take 4–5 minutes.

Done.

CHICKEN MAKHANI—leftovers...

Got a little chicken makhani leftover? You can make another meal the following night. I am showing you what to do if you have enough chicken for one or two to eat. The addition of rice will then serve 3–4. Garnish with boiled egg, cilantro, red bell pepper, and/or onion and glory in creating a whole new dish...

Serves: 3–4
Preparation time: 2–3 minutes + leftover chicken makhani (p. 90)
Cooking time: 20 minutes
Notes: Use any leftover chicken dish in this way to make another meal the next day.
Serving suggestion: With a raita (see "Accompaniments" section).
M/A: Yes. However, best when eaten immediately.
* No

	leftover chicken makhani recipe, approximately 2 cups (see previous page)
1 ¹/₂	cups basmati rice, washed and drained
3	cups boiling water
	garnish: cilantro, red onion, boiled egg... whatever you like

- Heat the leftover chicken in a pan over a medium flame.

- Add the rice, mix, and coat all the grains with the chicken and the sauce for a minute or two.

- Pour in the boiling water, stir once, cover with a lid, and turn the heat to medium low.

- Allow the rice to cook for 10 minutes, remove the lid, stir once, replace the lid, turn off the heat, and ignore for a further 10 minutes.

- Fluff the rice with a fork.

- Garnish.

Done.

PALAAK CHICKEN (SPINACH AND CHICKEN)

this protein + this vegetable + these spices + a dollop of yogurt + a hunk of bread = total nutrition

Serves: 6 as a side dish
Preparation time: 20 minutes
Cooking time: 40 minutes
Notes: This recipe is the same as that used for palaak paneer (see "Vegetables" section).
Try cubes of lamb as an alternative to the chicken.
At the time of pureeing the spinach leaves, I occasionally add a hefty knob of butter and ½ cup of heavy/double/whipping cream if I am feeling indulgent and want a richer and silkier finish.
Serving suggestion: With chapattis (see "Breads" section) and a raita (see "Accompaniments" section).
M/A: Yes. Just heat before serving.
* Yes

3	tablespoons canola oil
1	medium onion, sliced
1	tablespoon cumin seeds
1	tablespoon fresh ginger, grated
1	teaspoon salt
2	teaspoons garam masala
2	teaspoons turmeric
½	teaspoon red chili powder
2	tomatoes, sliced **OR** 1 cup chopped/crushed tomatoes (canned is ideal here)
2	bags spinach—approximately 9 ounces each, washed and drained

chicken:

2	pounds chicken breasts (approximately), diced into 2″ pieces
2	tablespoons canola oil
1	teaspoon salt
1	teaspoon garam masala
½	teaspoon red chili powder

- Heat the oil in a pan and add the onion, cumin seeds, and ginger. Cook over a medium heat for 5 minutes or so. Stir regularly.

- Add the salt, garam masala, turmeric, and chili powder, mix well, and cook for another 2–3 minutes—do not allow to burn.

- Now put in the tomatoes and allow the contents of the pan to blend and cook together for a further 8–10 minutes. Mix at intervals.

- Lay the spinach leaves over the tomato mixture. Cover the pan. (If all the leaves do not fit, add more gradually as the leaves cook and wilt down.) Allow to cook, remembering to stir the contents every 3–4 minutes. This step should take 15–20 minutes.

- Using a handheld, electric blender, cream the spinach into a smooth puree (just do this in the pan itself) and cook for 5 more minutes, or feel free not to blend and to leave the spinach in its wilder state.

- Meanwhile, heat 2 tablespoons canola oil in a frying pan over a medium/high flame. Add the chicken and sprinkle in the salt, garam masala, and red chili powder. Keep mixing to prevent sticking. It should take 8–10 minutes until the chicken is cooked (you should see no pink when you cut into a piece).

- Add the prepared chicken to the prepared spinach and heat through.

Done.

LAMB CHOPS, AMCHUR WALE (MANGO-SPICED)

If these chops do not get your juices going, then nothing will. You will need a bib, a pile of napkins, and not much else. This is one of my most adored auntie's recipes. As a rule, she makes a panful whenever I visit Newcastle and kindly honors my wish to be her sole and salacious invitee (it is truly a travesty if I hear her doorbell ring). The mango does not fall too far from the tree...my daughter, India, is quite the lady but rapidly morphs into a finger-licking, grease-smeared, gluttonous image of gorgeousness when she gets hold of (and does not let go of) these tangy chops.

Serves: 4
Preparation time: 5 minutes
Cooking time: 30 minutes
Notes: Cook the lamb to your desired preference—I like it well-done.
Serving suggestion: All by themselves.
M/A: Yes. However, best when eaten immediately.
* No

4	tablespoons salted butter
$^1/_2$–1	teaspoon salt (to taste)
2	tablespoons black pepper
10–12	lamb lollipop chops
3	tablespoons mango powder
	juice of a fresh lemon

- Over a low/medium heat, melt the butter in a large shallow frying pan.

- Add $^1/_2$ teaspoon salt and the pepper and stir for 3–4 minutes—do not allow to burn.

- Turn the heat up to medium/high and add the lamb. Stir every 2–3 minutes while allowing the lamb to sear and brown—takes about 15 minutes.

- Turn the heat to low, put on a lid, and leave for 5 minutes.

- Remove the lid, stir in the mango powder and lemon juice, and cook for a further 5 minutes. Taste the juices and add another $^1/_2$ teaspoon of salt if need be.

Done.

LAMB CURRY

As "THE" Nigella Lawson might entice...

My eyes are closed. I am transporting myself. I am being fanned by peacock feathers. I am draped in vibrant silks. My limbs are decked with precious gems. I am surrounded by plush cushions and opulence. The air I breathe hints of incense and fragrant oils. My tummy is flat...well, a girl can dream, can she not? This is one of those dishes that conjures up images of grandeur, fantasy, and elegance. It is a Punjabi curry heavily influenced by Mughalai, Muslim cuisine—rich in both spice and bold flavors. Make a robust base, splurge on your lamb, toast the naan bread—with one taste, you will be forgiven if your royal mind, too, begins to wander...

Serves: 8 as a side dish, 4 as a main dish
Preparation time: Preparing Masala 1 (p. xxxviii)
Cooking time: Approximately 90 minutes
Notes: I am loosely referring to this dish as a "curry," indicating the Western notion of a deeply flavored "saucy" dish. You will notice that no curry powder (a commercially prepared mixture of spices) is used as most Indian homes do not utilize this ingredient.
If you use lollipop chops, increase the number to 12 and decrease the final stage of cooking time from 50 minutes to about 20 minutes.
Serving suggestion: With store-bought naan bread and a raita (see "Accompaniments" section).
M/A: Yes. I find this tastes even better the following day.
* Yes

1	portion of prepared Masala 1 (p. xxxviii)
1/2	teaspoon salt
1/2	teaspoon red chili powder
8	lamb loin chops (approximately 2″ thickness)
2–3	cups boiling water as needed
	a handful of cilantro, chopped—to garnish

- Heat the prepared Masala 1 in a large shallow pan over a medium flame. Add the salt and red chili powder to the mix.

- Turn the heat up to medium/high, add the lamb chops, and sear the meat on both sides. This will take about 10 minutes.

- Add 2 cups of boiling water, stir, put on a lid, turn the heat to low/medium, and leave for 20 minutes. (Stir once or twice to check there is no sticking—adjust the temperature and add a little more boiling water if needed.)

- Remove the lid and cook for a further 50 minutes or so, stirring occasionally and adding water if needed.

- Garnish with cilantro.

  Done.

LAMB CURRY WITH CHANA DAL (WITH GRAM DAL/LENTILS)

You will follow the previous recipe but begin by soaking about **2 cups of chana dal** in cold water the night before. Wash and drain the dal well before adding to the seared lamb and coat well with the tomato and spice paste.

Next add the boiling water, cover, and simmer on a low heat. You may add **a cinnamon stick** here and **a black cardamom pod (cracked open)** as there is a little more to flavor than in the original recipe. I use lamb chops or boneless lamb depending upon what is available. Additional boiling water may be required to allow the lentils to cook. Leave the lid on the pot for the whole cooking time—this will force the lentils to soften. The result is always the same... lovely, lovely lamb.

LAMB ROGAN JOSH

The Mughals, whose cuisine is Persian-inspired, brought this dish to the cooler climate and high altitudes of Kashmir (mountainous North India). "Rogan" refers to the rich, red color while "josh" is all about passion. This version is a variation on the traditional...mine is yogurt-based, and I do not grind dry chilis or use saffron to create a red paste and color as many do. Let us consider this to be a Punjabi interpretation of the original recipe. Hot, spicy, and brimming with passion—now, with whom to share this aromatic, Himalayan dish?

Serves: 6
Preparation time: 10 minutes
Cooking time: 1 hour (perhaps a little more)
Notes: Make life easy—ask your butcher to dice the lamb for you. While s/he is at it, know that I always ask for the excess fat to be removed too.

If you get news of an unexpected guest or two, simply peel and quarter 2–3 small potatoes and add to the pan before you pour in the boiling water. You may need to add a little more water as all continues to cook, but you will have stretched the rogan josh to feed a few more delighted mouths.

Spoon out the whole, dried herbs before serving.
Serving suggestion: With any bread or rice and a carrot salad (see "Accompaniments" section).
M/A: Yes. It tastes even better the following day.
* Yes

4	tablespoons canola oil
2	black cardamoms (cracked open)
4	green cardamoms (cracked open)
4	cloves
2"–3"	cinnamon stick
4	black peppercorns
2	tablespoons cumin seeds
1	medium onion, finely sliced
1 ½–2	pounds boneless leg of lamb, diced into 2″ pieces (approximately)
2	teaspoons salt
1 ½	tablespoons garam masala
1 ½–2	teaspoons red chili powder
½	teaspoon fennel seeds
2	dried bay leaves
½	cup chopped/crushed tomatoes (canned is ideal here)
1 ½	cups boiling water (approximately)
½	cup plain yogurt—I use whole-milk in this recipe
	a handful of cilantro, chopped—to garnish

- Gently heat the oil in a wide, shallow pan over a medium flame.

- Add the black cardamoms, green cardamoms, cloves, cinnamon, peppercorns, and cumin seeds—heat for about a minute and do not allow to burn.

- Stir in the onion and cook for 8–10 minutes. Mix from time to time.

- Turn the heat to medium/high and introduce the chunks of lamb—sear, stir, and brown on all sides for 7–8 minutes.

- Sprinkle in the salt, garam masala, red chili powder, fennel seeds, and bay leaves. Mix and cook the spices and lamb for a further 2 minutes.

- Add the tomatoes and turn the heat to a medium flame. Stir from time to time for 5 minutes or so.

- Pour in the boiling water and bring the contents of the pan to a boil.

- Now, cover the pot and turn the heat to low/medium for about 40 minutes. (Occasionally check that there is ample liquid in the pot to prevent sticking and adjust accordingly—otherwise, leave it alone.)

- After 40 minutes, mix in the yogurt, heat through thoroughly, taste for salt, and add a little to taste if need be.

- Garnish with cilantro.

Done.

MEATBALLS

Italian, Turkish, Greek, or American—no matter where your balls come from, they should know how to hit the spot. Try this Indian version and I think you will find that they do just that.

Serves: 6–8
Preparation time: 20 minutes + Masala 1 (p. xxxviii)
Cooking time: 30 minutes
Notes: I know that it is usual in the West to cook one's meatballs first and then add them to the sauce—I am sure that would work too. I am just showing you the way my mum does it.
Serving suggestion: With kaju pulau (see "Rice" section) and a red onion salad (see "Accompaniments" section).
M/A: Yes. Just heat before serving.
* Yes

2	pounds ground lamb
3/4	teaspoon salt
2	tablespoons garam masala
2	tablespoons cumin seeds
1	teaspoon red chili powder
3	tablespoons dried fenugreek leaves
1	portion of prepared Masala 1 (p. xxxviii)
	a handful of cilantro, chopped—to garnish

- Using your hands, knead together the ground lamb and all of the dried spices in a large bowl—be sure that it is mixed well.

- Take about 2 tablespoons of meat at a time and make tightly shaped round balls. Rub your hands with a little canola oil to prevent the mix from sticking to your hands while forming the meatball if need be. Lay on a tray and put aside. The mixture will yield approximately 24 meatballs.

- Heat the already prepared Masala 1 in a wide, shallow pan over a medium flame and gently place the meatballs into the same pan. Try to avoid the balls touching one other.

- After 5 minutes, using a wooden spoon, turn the balls with care—they will keep their shape if you are patient. Leave for 2–3 more minutes before stirring once again then put on the lid, turn the heat down to low, and ignore for 10 minutes.

- Remove the lid, stir, replace the lid, switch off the heat, and leave for a further 10 minutes.

- Garnish with cilantro.

Done.

MEATBALL SUB... *Glorious!*

DHANIYA (CILANTRO) FISH

My mum never cooks fish—it makes her nervous—but she often uses this marinade on chicken. I tried it on cod one day, and the fish instantly screamed, "Eat me!" It is simply a show-stopper, so do not hold back and make it the star of your table. Serve with rice and something colorful—steamed carrots or grilled tomatoes would complete the picture.

Serves: 8–10
Preparation time: 15 minutes
Cooking time: 10–12 minutes
Notes: Try the marinade on chicken or lamb as an alternative.
Serving suggestion: With your favorite bread and kachumbar salad (see "Accompaniments" section) or mushroom pulau (see "Rice" section).
M/A: No. However, see the note below regarding freezing (*).
* No. However, if you are using a smaller amount of fish, you can freeze the extra marinade before it makes contact with the fish—do not waste your efforts.

2–3	big bunches of cilantro (approximately 6 cups, packed)
4–5	jalapeno peppers (you can test how hot you can go)
1 ¼	cups plain yogurt—I use whole-milk in this recipe
1	tablespoon salt
1	tablespoon black pepper
3	pounds white fish (I like cod or flounder)
3–4	tablespoons canola oil

- Chop the ends from the cilantro stems (cut off about 3") but keep the main part of the stalk on. Wash the herb thoroughly (immerse in running water) and drain off any excess water and dab with a paper towel. Place in a food processor.

- Chop off the top and bottom from the jalapeno peppers and add to the cilantro. (I would add the jalapeno peppers one at a time during the process if you are nervous about the heat—you know your own limit, or are about to find out!)

- Chop the cilantro and peppers in the processor. When the mix appears to stop moving, add ½ cup of yogurt to loosen the contents and stir carefully with a spoon if you are able. Pulse vigorously in the processor until a smooth green paste results. This whole process takes about 10 minutes. Transfer the contents to a large, flat, shallow dish.

- Now, add the remaining ¾ cup of yogurt, salt, and black pepper (again, gradually if you are unsure about the level of spice) and combine well. Taste—if too spicy, include a little more yogurt—then add the whole fillets of fish and smear all sides using your fingers. Cover and refrigerate for between 2–8 hours.

- Heat the oil in a large frying pan over a medium heat. Add the fish and fry for about 5 minutes on each side or until it is flaky and cooked through. Do not overcrowd the pan or else the fish will steam. Flip carefully. Cook the second side.

Done.

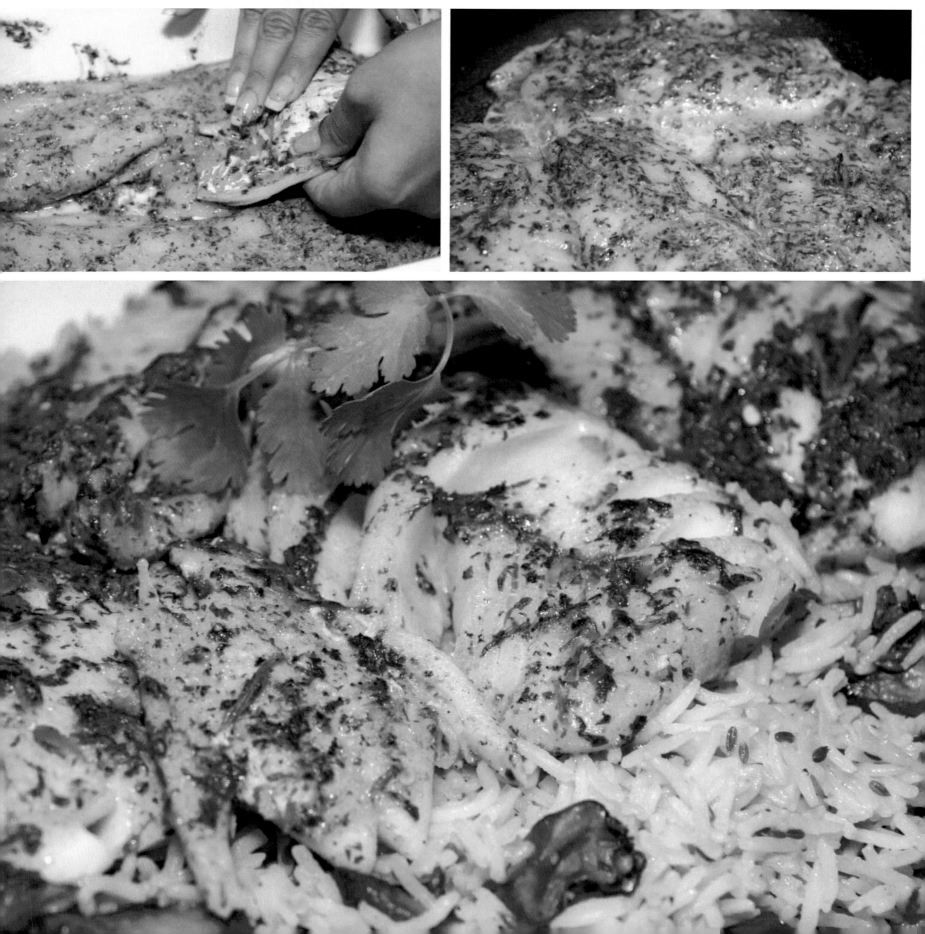

SPICED, BREADED FISH

The number of times I have fooled my son with this fillet of fish is not funny. He assumes he is having a crunchy chicken goujon, and instead he bites into a tilapia. The flavors in his mouth (and his eyes) just pop..."Mmm, this chicken is good!" Ha!

Serves: 4
Preparation time: 10 minutes
Cooking time: 6–8 minutes
Notes: Use any white fish.
A super tip—use one hand while coating with the "dry" ingredients (flour and breadcrumbs) and the other hand for dipping in the "wet" ingredient (egg)—less mess.
Serving suggestion: With bread and mayonnaise.
M/A: No
* No

In 3 separate, flat bowls:

1) $^3/_4$ cup all-purpose flour + $^1/_2$ teaspoon salt, combined well

2) 2 eggs, whisked + $^1/_2$ teaspoon salt, combined well

3) 1 cup store-bought, plain breadcrumbs + 2 teaspoons salt, 2 $^1/_2$ tablespoons garam masala, 2 $^1/_2$ tablespoons mango powder, 1 teaspoon red chili powder, combined well

4	tilapia fillets
$^1/_4$	cup canola oil for frying
	juice of a fresh lemon—to dress

- Prepare 3 flat bowls: **1)** flour and salt **2)** eggs and salt **3)** breadcrumbs and spices.

- Lay one piece of fish in the seasoned flour, flip, and make sure its whole area is coated.

- Lay the same piece of fish in the seasoned eggs, flip, and make sure its whole area is coated.

- Lay the egg-dipped fish in the seasoned breadcrumbs, flip, and really make sure the whole fish is evenly coated. Lay on a foil-lined tray.

- Repeat the flour, egg, and breadcrumb steps with each fillet.

- Now, heat the oil in a large frying pan over medium heat for a minute or so—do not allow it to burn.

- Carefully place each piece into the pan (you will notice bubbles around the browning edge of the fish), flip after about 3 minutes, and continue cooking on the other side for close to a further 3 minutes before you remove the fish from the pan. Squeeze the fresh lemon juice over the finished fish.

Done.

RICE...

WHITE RICE

A staple in many homes but it is imperative that you master how to make it—properly. It is not difficult, I promise. After all, nobody savors soggy, sticky, or undercooked rice. Although my mouth visibly waters at the thought of a dreamy Parmesan risotto, most Indians of my parents' generation and older simply cannot contemplate the idea of rice being "al dente" or creamy. To them, it just does not make sense. The point is that each grain of cooked rice in this recipe should be individual, dry, and yet soft to the touch.

Serves: 4
Preparation time: 2 minutes
Cooking time: 20 minutes
Notes: As a garnish you might heat 1 tablespoon of canola oil and 2 tablespoons of salted butter over a medium flame, add 1 cup of sliced, unsalted almonds (or any nut for that matter), and 1 teaspoon of sugar. Allow the nuts to brown and caramelize then sprinkle over the cooked rice—you just made white rice a little more memorable.
Serving suggestion: With any "saucy" dish. See "Lentils" section or "Poultry" section for ideas.
M/A: Yes. However, best when eaten immediately.
* No

2	cups basmati rice
4	cups cold water
$1/2$	teaspoon salt

- Thoroughly wash the rice under running water. Be sure to aggressively swish the grains about using your hand so as to loosen any dirt particles hanging around. Drain in a sieve.

- Put the drained rice into a pan.

- Add 4 cups of cold water and the salt.

- Bring the water to a boil, cover the pan, turn the heat to low/medium—do not stir. Turn down the heat if the water looks like it may boil over and leave over the flame for 10 minutes.

- Switch off the heat, remove the lid, stir gently, replace the lid, and leave for a further 10 minutes.

- Fluff the rice with a fork and serve.

  Done.

MATTAR PULAU (RICE WITH PEAS)

A "pulau" (you may see it as pilau, pilav, pilaf, palaw, or some such variation) is rice that has been coated with fat and then cooked in seasoned broth—usually with onions, vegetables, and/or meat. Kargil says this is the best thing he has ever eaten in his whole, entire life. He is mad about the nutty cumin seeds, the sweet peas, and buttery onions, and he yearns for this dish when he is tired or has just lost his soccer match—it seems to make everything okay. It is a super quick fix when time is limited and you have to raid the freezer or pantry. Serve with some plain yogurt and some store-bought Indian mango pickle—you are set.

Serves: 6
Preparation time: 5 minutes
Cooking time: 35 minutes
Notes: This rice, when leftover, heats up well when splashed with water and put in the microwave.
For a dinner, always prepare just before you want to eat or have simmering while your guests are enjoying their first drink.
I occasionally add a hefty knob of butter with the boiling water if I am looking for a silkier finish—the warm grains of rice will glisten.
Serving suggestion: With any lentil dish that interests you (see "Lentils" section) or plain yogurt.
M/A: Yes. However, best when eaten immediately.
* No

4	tablespoons canola oil
1	tablespoon cumin seeds
1	medium onion, finely sliced
2	cups frozen peas
2	cups basmati rice (washed well and drained)
1	teaspoon salt
4	cups boiling water

- Heat the oil over a medium flame.

- Add the cumin seeds and onion and cook for 5 minutes until soft. Stir to prevent sticking.

- Introduce the peas and cook for a further 2–3 minutes and then mix in the rice and salt. Coat each grain with the oil by stirring gently.

- Pour in the boiling water, bring the pot to a boil, cover the pan, turn the heat to low/medium—do not stir. Turn down the heat if the water looks like it may boil over and leave over the flame for 12–13 minutes.

- Switch off the heat, remove the lid, stir gently, replace the lid, and leave for a further 15 minutes.

- Fluff the rice with a fork and serve.

Done.

MUSHROOM PULAU
(RICE WITH MUSHROOMS)

Proceed from the previous recipe but add **¹/₂ pound sliced mushrooms** in place of the peas. Sauté for 3–4 minutes and follow the same directions.

KAJU PULAU
(RICE WITH CASHEW NUTS)

Proceed from the previous recipe but use **1 cup unsalted cashew nuts** in place of the peas. Throw in **a black cardamom (cracked open)** if you so desire as the flavor goes very well with the nuts. Follow the same directions.

TOMATO AND VEGETABLE PULAU

Serves: 6
Preparation time: 5 minutes
Cooking time: 35 minutes
Notes: This rice, when leftover, heats up well when splashed with water and put in the microwave.

For a dinner, always prepare just before you want to eat or have simmering while your guests are enjoying their first drink.

I occasionally add a hefty knob of butter with the boiling water if I am looking for a silkier finish—the warm grains of rice will glisten.

A super and colorful potluck offering as this rice is ideal when eaten at room temperature too.

Serving suggestion: With a raita (see "Accompaniments" section).

M/A: Yes, if to be eaten at room temperature.
* No

Follow the rice recipe for mattar pulau (p. 116) but add **2 cups frozen mixed vegetables** instead of the frozen peas. Sprinkle in **1 tablespoon turmeric** and **1 teaspoon red chili powder (optional)**, throw in **2 tomatoes, sliced**, and use the same directions.

CHICKEN BIRYANI

History reveals that biryani was brought to India by Persian travelers and merchants around the time of the Mughal Empire. It is viewed as a fine dish because it traditionally calls for exotic spices and expensive cuts of meat, and the whole meal is slow-cooked in order to achieve tender, melt-in-your-mouth morsels of lamb, goat, or chicken. The meat and rice are prepared separately and then assembled to create a balance of richly seasoned meat and grains. I read that nomads would bury a clay pot full of meat, rice, and spices in a fire pit. After time the pot was dug up and there appeared (almost magically) the steaming biryani. I am orchestrating a slightly easier method and version. I promise, its aroma, flavor, and texture will tease all of your senses...

Serves: 8–10
Preparation time: Chicken (marinate the night before) + 10 minutes
Cooking time: 75 minutes or so
Notes: There are many steps in preparing this dish so it helps to read through and be organized beforehand.
I have made biryani using lamb chops and boneless lamb too—both work well in place of the chicken.
You may have to do ¹/₂ a batch of the chicken at a time as there is a lot of chicken to sear. I do.
Serving suggestion: Serve with plain yogurt and a green salad. This is a meal in itself.
M/A: Yes, but only 30 minutes or so ahead of time. However, you could prepare the chicken and onions earlier, the rice too, and assemble and bake the dish just before your guests arrive.
* No

4	pounds chicken (approximately)—marinated. See chicken tikka recipe for marinade on p. 86 (I use perhaps 5 or 6 legs and 5 or 6 thighs—bone in, no skin). Prepare and refrigerate the night before.
3 ¹/₂	cups basmati rice, washed well
8	cups cold water
1 ¹/₂	teaspoons salt + ¹/₂ teaspoon salt + ¹/₄ teaspoon salt
4	tablespoons canola oil + 4 tablespoons canola oil
2	tablespoons cumin seeds
4	cloves
1	black cardamom (cracked open)
4	green cardamoms (cracked open)
3″	cinnamon stick
4	medium-sized onions, sliced into ¹/₄″ rings—divided in 2 parts
¹/₈	teaspoon saffron threads soaked in ¹/₂ cup hot milk (for 20 minutes or so)
1	teaspoon brown sugar

- Place the rice and water in a pan (with 1 ¹/₂ teaspoon salt and a black cardamom for extra fragrance if you wish) and bring the water to a boil. Allow to boil for 6 minutes only. Remove the pot from the stove, pour off the hot water, and immediately fill with cold tap water in order to stop the rice from cooking any further. Drain into a sieve and leave aside.

- In another pan, heat the oil over a medium flame in a large, shallow pan and add the cumin seeds, cloves, cardamoms, and cinnamon. Allow the release of flavors for 2–3 minutes. Stir and do not allow to burn.

- Put in half of the onions and ¹/₂ teaspoon salt. Cook over medium/high heat for 8 minutes or so until they are soft and golden.

(continued...)

- Mix in the chicken, stir regularly, and sear and brown all sides for 10 minutes or so. (I often do half a batch of the chicken at a time due to shortness of space.) Fish out the cloves, cardamoms, and cinnamon if the idea of catching one between your teeth abhors you.

- If you did sear the chicken in two separate batches, now it is time to combine all of the seared chicken close together in the base of the pan.

- Retrieve the sieve and spoon the half-cooked rice over the chicken.

- Drizzle the saffron-infused milk over the rice.

- Seal the pot with foil, place on a tight-fitting lid, and put the whole pan into a preheated oven (400°F) on the middle shelf for 50 minutes.

- Meanwhile, brown the other half of the onions with 4 tablespoons canola oil, $1/4$ teaspoon salt, and 1 teaspoon brown sugar until the onions are caramelized and oozing sweetness (about 15–20 minutes over medium/high heat—keep stirring).

- When the timer pings, remove the biryani from the oven and wait for up to 30 minutes, or unveil the steaming pot, dress with the caramelized onions, and dig right in.

Done.

BREADS...

DRESSED-UP PITA

Beginning with a store-bought naan or pita bread is not cheating...consider it something like wriggling into those "Spanx" before getting dressed for a night out. We all have to start somewhere.

In a bowl, mix together **a handful of chopped cilantro**, ¹⁄₄ **teaspoon salt**, **1 teaspoon red chili flakes (optional)**, and **4 tablespoons canola oil**. Lightly broil store-bought **naan** or **pita bread** for about 4 minutes under a medium heat (do each side), remove from the oven, and brush the topside with the seasoned oil (right up to the edges), place under the broiler for an additional minute or so—keep an eye on it as this can easily burn.

Done.

Slice straight away and serve warm alongside any dish or simply as an appetizer.

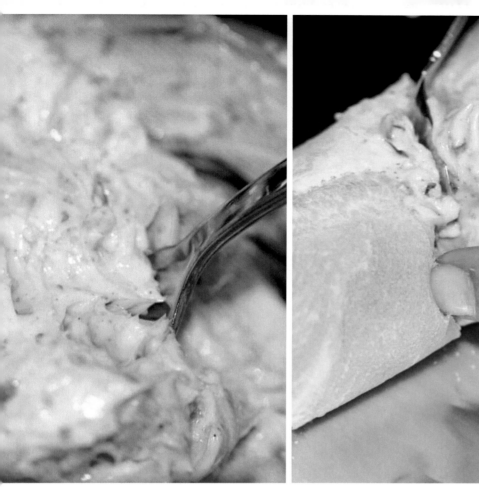

SEASONED BUTTER, PUNJABI STYLE

Allow approximately **8 tablespoons salted butter** to soften at room temperature. Add ¼ **teaspoon salt**, **teaspoon garam masala**, and **2 tablespoons of finely chopped cilantro**. Mush together with a fork. Refrigerate for up to a week or use immediately.

Take **a baguette**, slice at 2″ intervals (almost to the base but not quite—this keeps the bread in one piece and therefore easier to manage). Spoon a teaspoon of seasoned butter between each slice, spread on the inside surface, wrap the whole baguette in foil, and pop into the pre-heated oven (350° F) for 8–10 minutes.

Unwrap the warm bread, tear off a slice, savor, savor, savor...

(Spread this butter on toast or naan bread, or allow it to bathe your warm, cooked corn on the cob.)

ATTA DOUGH
(basic dough for most homemade Indian breads)

Preparation time: 5–10 minutes
Cooking time: N/A
Notes: Use as a base for later recipes (I will tell you where).
Serving suggestion: N/A
M/A: Yes. I make up to 24 hours in advance.
* No

Take **4 cups atta flour** (whole-wheat if you like). Gradually add about **2 cups cold tap water** and **1 tablespoon canola oil** as you mix with fingers. Knead well using your knuckles and a little bit of effort—4–5 minutes or so.

Add a little extra water or atta flour as needed to create a soft but firm dough—it should not be sticky. Refrigerate for 30 minutes and up to 24 hours before using—any longer and it may "loosen" or lose its firmness.

Done.

CHAPATTI/ROTI (FLATBREAD)

When my mum first arrived in Newcastle, she had no idea how to peel a potato let alone champion a chapatti. Initially, she was too embarrassed to tell her mother-in-law, so my dad would sneak into the kitchen, make the dough, and roll out a mountain of rotis for the whole family. She did not take the credit for long as her secret was soon found out, but my uncle, too, brought home a new bride and my auntie (an expert with breads) was more than happy to step in while my mum took over the meat, lentils, and vegetables. It is said that if a chapatti inflates while being prepared then the person for whom it is intended is hungry...and what a gratifying feeling it is to satiate that need. (This takes practice so do not fret—just be prepared to accept whatever comes your way. Inflation, in this case, is a bonus!) I make these every couple of weeks, and my family has learned to wait patiently—sometimes extremely patiently.

Serves: Makes 12–15 rotis
Preparation time: 2 minutes + prepared atta dough (p. 128)
Cooking time: 3 minutes (approximately) per chapatti
Notes: A "tava" is a flat, sideless surface used for making chapattis. Use a flat-bottomed frying pan if you do not have a "tava."
(Always be prepared to test one or two first to get the temperature of the vessel just right—my mum still does that today. My dad, however, gets it right the first time—every time!)

1	portion of prepared atta dough (p. 128)
2	cups loose atta flour to help with consistency and rolling
	knobs of salted butter for serving (optional)

Serving suggestion: With any vegetable, lentil, or meat dish.
M/A: No. A very experienced Indian home cook (that is, a grandma) can make ahead, but mine never ever stay soft enough to eat later.
* No

- Heat a "tava" (flat, sideless surface used for making chapattis and other breads) or a flat-bottomed frying pan over a medium flame for 2–3 minutes.

- Take about ¼-cup-size ball from the prepared atta dough and roll in the atta flour (this prevents sticking) and flatten the ball using your thumbs.

- Roll on a dry board or kitchen surface to approximately 7″ in diameter—size does not really matter (in this instance anyway). The roti should not be more than 2 mm thick. Dip in the flour again if too sticky but try to brush off the excess loose flour with your fingers as this causes the chapatti to brown before it is actually cooked.

- Place on the hot surface for about 60 seconds—notice how the center and edges begin to darken slightly (it is cooking) and some parts of the roti may rise. Turn over for another 60 seconds or so.

- Carefully flip over once more—you will see spots of brown on the surface. Take a clean hand towel and lightly press down firmly but gently on the edges and center to encourage the roti to inflate (it may or may not), and ensure all parts are getting an equal amount of heat (another 60 seconds or thereabouts). Flip once more for a few seconds if you are looking for a little more color.

- Smother the top with butter (optional).

Done.

PARANTHA (BUTTERY FLATBREAD)

A denser, more buttery version of the chapatti.

Serves: Makes 8–10 paranthas
Preparation time: 2–3 minutes + prepared atta dough (p. 128)
Cooking time: 3–4 minutes (approximately) per parantha
Notes: A "tava" is a flat, sideless surface used for making chapattis. Use a flat-bottomed frying pan if you do not have a "tava."
I melt a little butter in the microwave as needed for this recipe.
Serving suggestion: With any vegetable, lentil, or meat dish.
M/A: No
* No

1	portion of prepared atta dough (p. 128)
2	cups loose atta flour to help with consistency and rolling
5–6	tablespoons melted, salted butter (or canola oil) knobs of salted butter for serving

- Heat a "tava" (flat, sideless surface used for making breads) or a flat-bottomed frying pan over a medium/high flame for 2–3 minutes.

- Take about ⅓-cup-size ball from the prepared atta dough and roll in the atta flour (this prevents sticking) and flatten the ball using your thumbs.

- Roll on a dry board or kitchen surface to approximately 7″ in diameter. The dough should not be more than 3 mm thick. Dip in the flour again if too sticky but try to brush off the excess loose flour with your fingers as this causes the parantha to brown before it is cooked.

- Brush the whole disk of dough with melted butter (or canola oil).

- Fold the circle in half and brush the topside with melted butter.

- Fold into a quarter circle.

- Dip in the loose atta flour on both sides and once again brush off the excess flour.

- Roll on the board to 2–3 mm thickness—it will naturally form a triangular shape.

- Place on the hot surface for 60 seconds or so.

- Flip over for a further 60 seconds and brush the slightly cooked side with more butter (right up to the edges).

- Flip again to finish cooking the buttered side (about 45 seconds) and brush the unbuttered side (right up to the edges). Press down with a spatula to ensure uniform cooking.

- Flip for the final time (last 45 seconds), remove from the heat, and serve with a knob of melting butter on top.

Done.

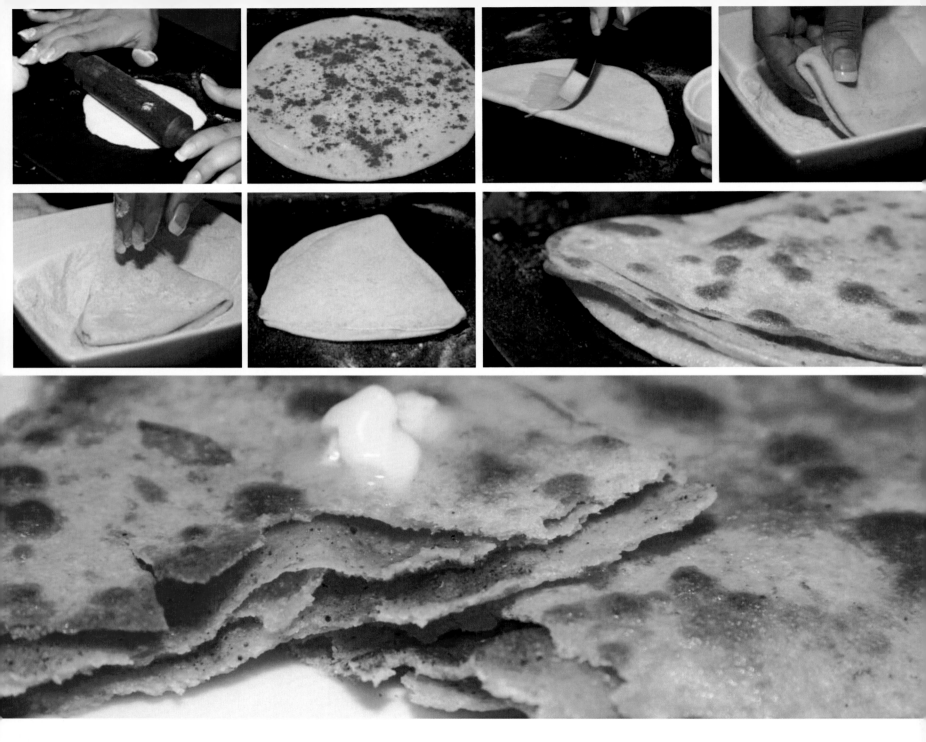

SEASONED PARANTHA
(SEASONED, BUTTERY FLATBREAD)

See prior page for the basic version—after buttering the round of dough, equally distribute ¹⁄₈ **teaspoon salt**, ¹⁄₄ **teaspoon garam masala**, and ¹⁄₈ **teaspoon red chili powder** over the surface. Cook as in the previous recipe. The folds will catch all the drips of salted butter...nothing wasted!

STUFFED PARANTHA (STUFFED FLATBREAD)

The Punjab's answer to the calzone. Experiment with a variety of fillings to find your preference or prepare a couple of them and allow the family to choose. This was a weekend morning brunch for us growing up. It takes time, though. I remember we were usually finished by the time my mum reached the table. She soon got sick of that and later learned to half-cook the paranthas (without fat) before we all sat down and once we did she would rapidly complete the cooking of them on the hot pan. She always tops them off with a hefty knob of butter...let it ooze.

Serves: Makes 10–12 stuffed paranthas
Preparation time: Your fillings (see p. 138 for ideas) + prepared atta dough (p. 128)
Cooking time: 3–4 minutes (approximately) per parantha
Notes: A "tava" is a flat, sideless surface used for making chapattis. Use a flat-bottomed frying pan if you do not have a "tava."
I melt a little butter in the microwave as needed for this recipe.
The filling should not hold too much moisture—look over the page for some suggestions.
Serving suggestion: With plain yogurt.
M/A: Yes. Heat on the "tava" or in a frying pan over a low/medium flame just before serving.
* No

1	portion of prepared atta dough (p. 128)
2	cups loose atta flour to help with consistency and rolling
	filling(s) of choice—about ⅓ cup per parantha (see p. 138)—at room temperature
5–6	tablespoons melted, salted butter (or canola oil) knobs of salted butter for serving (optional)

- Heat a "tava" (flat, sideless surface used for making breads) or a flat-bottomed frying pan over a medium flame for 2–3 minutes.

- Take about ⅓-cup-size ball from the prepared atta dough and roll in the atta flour (this prevents sticking) and flatten the ball using your thumbs.

- Roll on a board or kitchen surface to approximately 7″ in diameter. However, the dough should not be more than 2 mm thick. Dip in the flour again if it is too sticky but try to brush off the excess loose flour with your fingers as too much flour causes the dough to brown before it is cooked.

- Place about ⅓ cup of filling in the center of the disk, fold in the outer parts as the photographs show, flatten gently with your palm to secure all the folds, dip in the loose atta flour on both sides, and roll out to about a 5 mm thickness.

- Place on the hot surface and allow to cook for 90 seconds or so.

- Flip over for a further 90 seconds and brush the topside with melted butter (or canola oil).

- Flip again for 40 seconds or so (meanwhile butter the unbuttered topside) and flip for the last time (another 40 seconds). Press down the edges with a spatula if you feel the need.

- Remove from the heat.

- Put an optional (but suggested) knob of butter on top.

Done.

STUFFED PARANTHA—FILLINGS

Potato/alloo—to **boiled, mashed potato** add **finely chopped red onion, chopped cilantro, chopped jalapeno pepper (optional), salt, garam masala, red chili powder,** and **mango powder** to taste. *This is the most common filling for a parantha and by far my favorite. I'm drooling...*

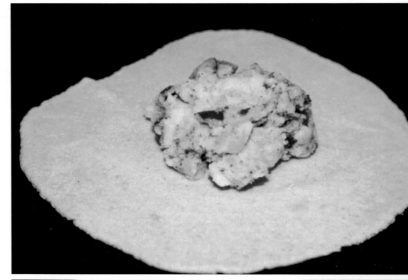

Keema—use the **keema** recipe (p. 10). *This is such a crowd pleaser—the only caveat being that, even now, I find them tedious to roll out for a lot of people, so I suggest you keep these for a very small gathering (or self) for your first few attempts—I still do.*

Paneer—if you have not used "paneer" before, learn a little about it in the "Spices and Herbs" section. Crumble the **paneer**, add **finely chopped red onion, chopped cilantro, chopped jalapeno pepper (optional), salt, garam masala, red chili powder,** and **mango powder** to taste. *Plain paneer and onion was how I introduced my children to this treat. I once resorted to feta cheese as I had forgotten to defrost my frozen paneer—not too bad at all.*

DAL PARANTHA (LENTIL-FLAVORED FLATBREAD)

A fatter, fuller-flavored chapatti. Fabulous.

Serves: Makes 10–12 dal paranthas
Preparation time: 5–8 minutes + leftover moong dal (p. 66)
Cooking time: 3–4 minutes (approximately) per parantha
Notes: A "tava" is a flat, sideless surface used for making chapattis. Use a flat-bottomed frying pan if you do not have a "tava."
A super, delicious way to use up leftover moong dal (p. 66).
Serving suggestion: With plain yogurt.
M/A: No
* No

4	cups atta flour
1	cup leftover moong dal (p. 66)—consistency does not matter for this recipe
1/2	small onion, finely chopped
2	tablespoons fresh ginger, finely grated
1	jalapeno pepper, finely chopped (optional)
	a handful of cilantro, finely chopped
2	teaspoons salt
2	tablespoons garam masala
1 1/2	teaspoons red chili powder
1	cup water (approximately), for kneading
2	cups loose atta flour to help with consistency and rolling
5–6	tablespoons melted, salted butter (or canola oil)
	knobs of salted butter for serving (optional)

- Using a little water at a time to bind and knead together all of the ingredients (except the last 3) and create a firm dough. This should take 4–5 minutes.

- Heat a "tava" (flat, sideless surface used for making breads) or a flat-bottomed frying pan over a medium/high flame for 2–3 minutes.

- Take about 1/3-cup-size piece of dough and roll out to approximately 7″ in diameter and 3–4 mm thick and place on the hot surface for 60 seconds or so.

- Flip over for a further 60 seconds and brush the topside with melted butter (or canola oil).

- Flip over for a further 50 seconds, brush the unbuttered side, and flip for the last 50 seconds.

- Put a knob of optional (but suggested) butter on top.

Done.

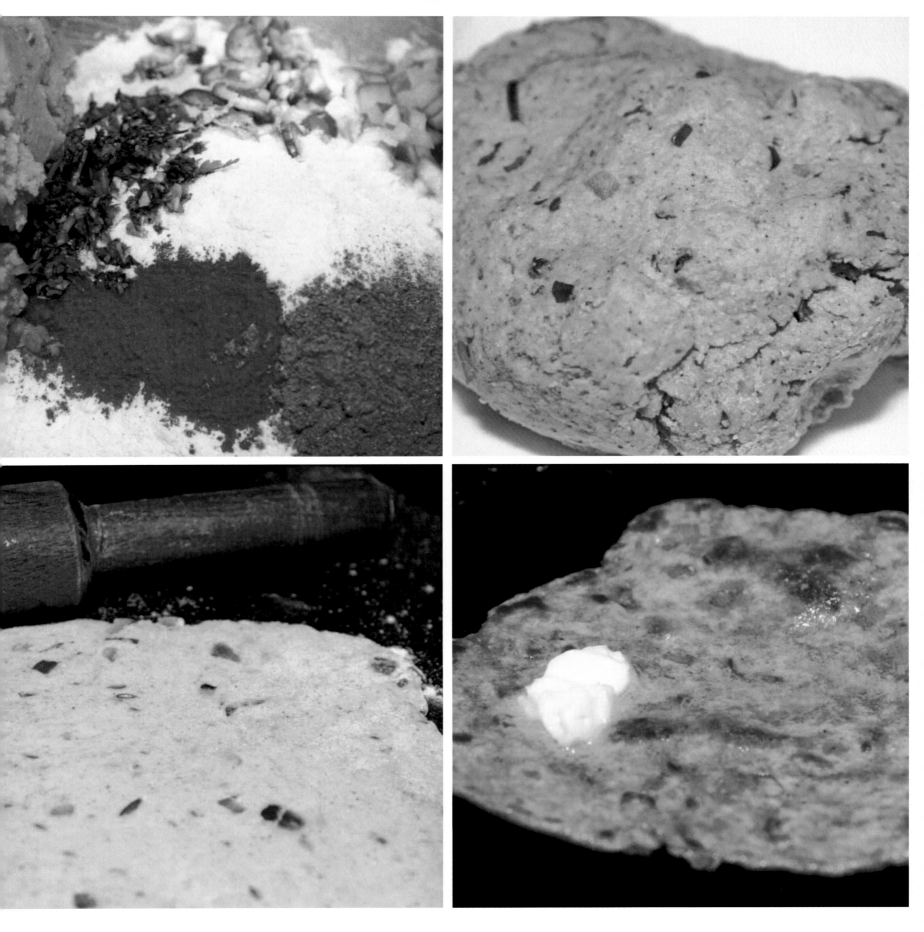

POORI (PUFFY BREAD)

Do not even attempt to eat these before your weekly weigh-in—simply accept as an enormous pleasure.

Serves: Makes about 12–15 pooris
Preparation time: 2 minutes + prepared atta dough (p. 128)
Cooking time: 2 minutes (approximately) per poori
Notes: Some season the dough with salt and/or carom seeds, but I refrain as the side dish is often amply flavorful.
Serving suggestion: With any "saucy" dish. A traditional option is to pair with alloo, thari wale (see "Vegetables" section—"alloo, poori" is a recurring answer to "What shall we serve for lunch?").
M/A: No
* No

1	portion of prepared atta dough (p. 128)
2	cups loose atta flour to help with consistency and rolling
	canola oil—enough for deep-frying, about 3″ deep

- Heat the oil in a wok or deep pan over a medium/high flame until you see bubbles at the edge of the pan (it takes about 5 minutes).

- Take about ¼-cup-size ball from the prepared atta dough and roll in the atta flour (this prevents sticking) and flatten the ball using your thumbs.

- Roll on a board or kitchen surface to approximately 5″ in diameter—it does not really matter but it is aesthetically pleasing to try and make all the pooris close to the same size (if you even care, that is). They should not be more than 2 mm thick. Try not to dip in the flour again as too much atta flour on the surface will cause the poori to brown before it is fully cooked.

- Gently place the disk of dough in the hot oil. Press down lightly with a spatula, then lift, then press. As you notice the underside browning, carefully flip over. Pushing down gently encourages the poori to inflate. This whole process should take 60–90 seconds. Be prepared to test the first couple of pooris as the oil being too hot will cause burning, and it being too cool will take away the desired crispiness. Adjust the flame accordingly.

- Drain on a paper towel or in a colander.

Done.

BHATURA (POTATO BREAD)

This potato bread is traditionally eaten with chana masala and is another example of New Delhi street food at its best. I never know if the vendor's plates are clean or if the water is safe to drink, but I tell you that fluffy, airy, pillowy carbs coupled with spicy chickpeas can override any germophobic fear I may have fleetingly had.

Serves: Makes 6–8 bhaturas
Preparation time: 10 minutes + boiling potato + 5 hours waiting
Cooking time: 2 minutes (approximately) per bhatura
Notes: I do not know the science behind the inclusion of the baking powder, but I do know that having included it and by allowing the dough to rest, you will return a more fluffy bread.
My auntie kneads and then leaves the dough out overnight (still unrefrigerated) and works with it the following day.
Serving suggestion: With chana masala (see "Lentils" section).
M/A: No
* No

2 ½	cups all-purpose flour
⅓	cup potato, boiled and mashed
1	teaspoon salt
1	teaspoon carom seeds
1	teaspoon baking powder
2	tablespoons dried fenugreek leaves (optional)
1	tablespoon canola oil
¾	cup plain yogurt—I use whole-milk or low-fat in this recipe
	canola oil—enough for deep-frying, about 3″ deep

- Mix together the flour, potato, salt, carom seeds, baking powder, fenugreek leaves, and a tablespoon of canola oil. Add the yogurt gradually as you knead the dough. This should take 4–5 minutes. Add a little extra flour or yogurt as needed so a firm dough results. Cover and put aside (not refrigerated) for 5 hours if possible.

- Heat the oil in a wok or deep pan over a medium/high flame for 4–5 minutes. Now turn the heat down to medium only.

- Take about ⅓-cup-size piece of dough (rub a little canola oil on your hands if the dough is too sticky—this helps) and roll into a traditional oval shape about 7″ in length with a 2–3 mm thickness (no thicker and avoid any holes). The dough is often difficult to handle—all I can say is that it is so for myself too. Try to be patient and oiling the workbench might also help to manipulate it. Pick it up before it sticks to the work area and lower cautiously into the hot oil.

- Press down gently, using a spatula, and flip carefully after 45 seconds or so. Press and release for a further 45 seconds, lift out, drain, and break into this deceivingly light bread. (Taste test the first one to see that the inside as well as the outside is cooked—adjust the temperature if need be.)

Done.

ACCOMPANIMENTS...

Raitas:

Salads:

Chutneys/sauces:

RAITA—cucumber

Yogurt is used as a coolant alongside many Indian dishes. It allows one to relish a spicy bite while balancing and offsetting the heat—the yogurt harmonizes the plate. It is perfectly acceptable to take a spoonful of yogurt with a spoonful of rice, to mix it with a vegetable dish, to use as a dip for kebabs, or as a cooling agent for a seasoned parantha (see "Breads" section). When a spice or flavoring is added to the yogurt it becomes a "raita." It is served chilled. Delicious and nutritious.

Serves: 8–10 as a condiment
Preparation time: 10 minutes
Cooking time: N/A
Notes: You can add all sorts of flavors to the raita. I know that the Persian kitchen adds raisins and walnuts to it, and Greek cuisine includes garlic. I have offered the typical, North Indian suggestions.
If you prefer not to add the fresh herbs, simply leave them out. The cucumber and black pepper offer enough taste. Greek yogurt is a super choice for raita.
Serving suggestion: As a condiment to any Indian dish.
M/A: Yes. I often make a day in advance.
* No

1	English cucumber
1	carton plain yogurt—approximately 2 pounds (I use whole-milk or low-fat but not fat-free, depending upon my mood)
¹/₂	teaspoon salt
¹/₂–1	teaspoon black pepper
	a huge handful of cilantro, chopped
	a handful of mint, chopped
¹/₄–¹/₂	cup milk (if needed)

- Onto a chopping board, grate the cucumber against the coarse-grating side of a box grater.

- Next, take small handfuls of the grated cucumber and squeeze over a bowl (if saving the cucumber juices to drink later—mix with chilled water—just a thought) or over the kitchen sink if discarding. Collect the squeezed out cucumber in a bowl. The idea is to retain as much of the flesh of the cucumber with as little of the juices as is possible. Squeeze hard!

- In another, larger mixing bowl and using a handheld whisk, mix together the yogurt, salt, and pepper.

- When the yogurt is smooth, fold in the fresh herbs and cucumber.

- Taste for salt. Adjust the seasoning as needed.

- Refrigerate.

  Done.

  (Before serving, you may find that the yogurt is too thick for your liking—just add a little cold milk to loosen it.)

RAITA—cucumber, red onion, and tomato

Follow the RAITA—cucumber recipe on the previous page and, alongside the cucumber, add:
2 tomatoes, chopped, and **a small red onion, finely chopped.**

Refrigerate to chill.
Done.

RAITA—mango and red onion

Another idea is to follow the RAITA—cucumber recipe on the previous page but omit the cucumber and include: **a small red onion, finely chopped** and **the diced flesh of a sweet mango** alongside the **cilantro** and **mint.**

Refrigerate to chill.
Done.

RAITA—potato

Serves: 8–10 as a condiment
Preparation time: 10 minutes (+ boiling the potato)
Cooking time: N/A
Serving suggestion: As a condiment to any Indian dish.
M/A: Yes. I often make a day in advance.
* No

After whisking together:

1	carton plain yogurt—approximately 2 pounds
¹/₂	teaspoon salt
¹/₂–1	teaspoon black pepper

fold in:

¹/₂	pound potatoes (previously peeled, boiled, and chopped into ¹/₂″ pieces)

Adding **a pinch of red chili powder** and/or **chopped cilantro** is your choice entirely.

Refrigerate to chill.
Done.

RAITA—boondi (dough balls)

Serves: 8–10 as a condiment
Preparation time: 5 minutes
Cooking time: N/A
Notes: Boondi are tiny fried balls of dough made from garbanzo bean flour—they are available in the packaged goods section of the Indian store only.
The boondi will expand and soften once mixed into the yogurt. Do not eat immediately—refrigerate to allow the latter to happen over an hour or so.
If you buy the spicy or "masala" boondi, omit the salt and the black pepper.
Serving suggestion: As a condiment to any Indian dish.
M/A: Yes. I make at least 1 hour in advance.
* No

After whisking together:

1	carton plain yogurt—approximately 2 pounds
¹/₂	teaspoon salt
¹/₂–1	teaspoon black pepper

fold in:

1	cup "boondi"/"bundi"

If the raita appears to be too thick for your liking, loosen with a little milk before serving.

Sprinkle with **chili flakes (optional).**

Refrigerate to chill.
Done.

RED ONION SALAD

Serves: 4–6 as a garnish
Preparation time: 5 minutes
Cooking time: N/A
Notes: If the onion is particularly strong, add $1/2$ teaspoon of sugar to the mix too.
Serving suggestion: As a garnish to almost anything.
M/A: Yes. However, no more than an hour ahead of serving.
* No

Finely slice **a large red onion**. Sprinkle over $1/2$ **teaspoon salt** and **1 teaspoon black pepper**. Squeeze over the **juice of 1 lemon** and throw in **a handful of finely chopped cilantro**. Toss well.

Done.

KACHUMBAR (MIXED) SALAD

A sure means to bring a lot of color and some cheerfulness to your plate.

Toss together the following list of ingredients:

1	English cucumber, diced		1	teaspoon salt
2	large tomatoes, diced		1	teaspoon black pepper
2	large carrots, peeled and diced			a handful of cilantro, chopped
¹/₂	red onion, chopped			juice of 2 lemons

Serve straight away. **Done.**

CARROT SALAD

This salad is so refreshing, and as an accompaniment, it brightens up almost any meal. I usually make it in the morning and refrigerate it so as to allow the dish to chill and for the spices to marry by the evening. I adopted the idea to present the salad on a layer of spinach leaves from a wonderful Thai restaurant in Atlanta. Vibrant, tangy, crunchy, and extremely light.

Serves: 6 as a side salad
Preparation time: No time at all if you buy pre-grated carrots
Cooking time: 3 minutes + 10 minutes cooling time + tossing time
Notes: I suggest 20 ounces of carrots as I have found that the 10-ounce pre-cut, matchstick or grated/shredded carrot bags are most readily available in stores.
Crush the nuts by placing them in a sealed Ziploc bag and smashing lightly with a rolling pin—save a tablespoon or so for garnishing if you like.
Also add chopped cilantro or thinly sliced red radishes if you happen to have them in the fridge.
Always make ahead, chill, and eat cold.
Serving suggestion: Alongside any dish that might benefit from some crunch or a pop of color.
M/A: Yes. However, best when served on the same day as it is prepared. Make ahead and chill for 3–4 hours.
* No

5	tablespoons canola oil
2	teaspoons mustard seeds
2	teaspoons cumin seeds
1	teaspoon salt
1	teaspoon black pepper
1	teaspoon sugar
	juice of 2 lemons
20	ounces grated carrots, approximately (see "Notes")
1	cup dry-roasted, salted peanuts—lightly crushed if you like (see "Notes")

- Heat the oil in a wide, shallow frying pan over medium/high heat for a minute or so.

- Add the mustard seeds and the cumin seeds. The seeds and oil will begin to spit. Continue to mix for 2–3 minutes as the seeds cook but be careful that they are not allowed to burn.

- Add the salt, pepper, sugar, and lemon juice. Mix well and remove the pan from the stove. Allow the contents to cool for 10 minutes or so.

- Toss in the carrots. Follow with the nuts. Combine well.

- Chill.

Done.

MINT CHUTNEY

A "chutney" (in the Indian sense of the word at least) is totally indiscriminate. It includes savory, sweet, dry, "saucy," and pickled condiments. When the Chopra family speaks of chutney, this is the first one that comes to mind. I cannot begin to describe the summer memories that this recipe brings back to me, my sister, and my cousins too. My paternal granddad would nurture the mint and tomatoes on his allotment and in his greenhouse. He would proudly stride home, laden with his treasures, and permit the grandchildren to tease off and prepare the precious leaves. He would set up his work station, roll up his sleeves, squat on the outside doorstep, and using his "kundi sota" (a hugely oversized stone pestle and mortar), he would begin to fuel the splashes, sloshes, scents, and anticipation that came with delivering this accompaniment. Our granddad was a gentle soul, sure of opinion, yet a being of few words. He was surrounded by strong and vocal women. As a child, I often contemplated what was perambulating his thoughts. I wonder if it was that, although the Chopra ladies knew how to conduct a home and a kitchen, they could only truly complete the evening meal with his most valuable donation.

Serves: 10–12 as a condiment
Preparation time: 20 minutes—perhaps a little more
Cooking time: N/A
Notes: Use a food processor for this recipe.
This will probably taste slightly different each time you prepare it as a result of the sweetness of the tomatoes/ onions or the intensity of the mint/serrano chilis.
The consistency will vary too—it is not an issue.
I buy mint in this quantity from the farmers' market—far more economical.
Some add the flesh of a sour apple or unripe mango to the mix for added tartness—I add extra pomegranate powder if need be.

Serving suggestion: Chilled.
Alongside chapatti (see "Breads" section) and moong/ mung dal (see "Lentils" section).
In a cheddar cheese sandwich. Fabulous!
Spoon a little chutney into mayonnaise or cream cheese to create a whole new dip.
M/A: Yes. It will keep in the refrigerator for up to a week.
* Yes. It may be on the watery side having been frozen, so just drain off what you can before you eat it.

4	very tightly packed cups (approximately) mint leaves and stems—remove the thicker, dark-colored, tough stems. Wash, drain, and dab the leaves and stems well with a hand towel to remove any excess water	2	medium-sized tomatoes, quartered
		¹/₂–1	serrano chili (begin with ¹/₂)
		1	tablespoon salt
		¹/₂	tablespoon black pepper
1	large onion, peeled and quartered	1	teaspoon red chili flakes
3″	piece of fresh, peeled ginger, roughly chopped	2¹/₂	tablespoons pomegranate powder

- Depending upon how big your food processor is, pack about half from the above ingredients into it. I usually have a big bowl and a wooden spoon at hand to help while I work in batches. As long as it all comes together in the end, there is no real order.

- The leaves and stems can be quite dense, so you may need to pause and use a spoon to help loosen the contents of the food processor as you work. This process may take longer than you anticipate it to.

- Gradually add more of the ingredients.

- As the chutney begins to evolve (and you have all of the ingredients and separate batches back in the food processor), test for the seasoning. Add more salt or the extra half of the serrano chili if you feel the need. Pulse once more. Taste test and adjust as required.

- Refrigerate.

Done.

TOMATO CHUTNEY

A homemade tomato sauce—punctuates any meal with a promise of flavor, color, and moisture.

Serves: 6–8 as a condiment
Preparation time: 10 minutes
Cooking time: 20 minutes + cooling time
Notes: Try to find tomatoes that are firm, ripe, but not too "juicy" as the chutney may become liquidy.
The tomatoes do not need to be peeled.
Liquidize until smooth or pulse to be as chunky as you like.
Add 1 teaspoon chili flakes, alongside the black pepper, if you would like to include some heat.
Serving suggestion: Chilled on toast or try heating and tossing with spaghetti and chopped cilantro.
M/A: Yes
* Yes

4	tablespoons canola oil
1	tablespoon cumin seeds
1	large onion, finely sliced
2	dried bay leaves
2"	cinnamon stick
4	cloves
1 1/2	teaspoons salt
1	teaspoon black pepper
1	teaspoon sugar
10	large, firm but ripe tomatoes (approximately 2– 2 1/2 pounds), roughly chopped

- Pour the oil into a large frying pan and heat for a minute or so over a medium flame.

- Add the cumin seeds, onion, bay leaves, cinnamon stick, and cloves, and cook for 5–6 minutes. Allow the onions to soften but not brown. Mix and adjust the flame as needed.

- Stir in the salt, black pepper, and sugar. Cook for 1 minute.

- Throw in the tomatoes, turn the heat up to medium/high, and mix occasionally as you cook for 10–12 minutes. Gently mash the tomatoes with the back of a wooden spoon—you will know when they are soft and cooked. Remove from the heat and leave to cool for 30 minutes or thereabouts.

- Pull out and discard the bay leaves, cinnamon stick, and cloves.

- Using a handheld, electric blender, pulse the ingredients to the desired consistency.

- Refrigerate.

Done.

DESSERTS...

GAJRELA (SWEET, SPICED CARROTS)

This cheery dessert is a classic conclusion to the end of any meal. Try to find particularly orange/red carrots as they are often the sweetest and most flavorful. The hot gajrela may be served as is, with a scoop of vanilla ice cream, or with a dollop of whipped cream as I have shown. This dessert takes time but is definitely worth the wait. If you look forward to a bite or two of carrot cake, this is the choice for you.

Serves: 6 if alongside ice cream
Preparation time: 5 minutes
Cooking time: 70–80 minutes
Notes: Buy store-bought, pre-grated/shredded carrots to make life easy. The prepared bags of carrots often come in 10-ounce packages—I use 2 bags and add an extra splash of milk to the recipe to make it all work.
Every time I prepare this dessert, my finished product looks different from the time before. Sometimes it appears a little creamy, sometimes more brown in color, but I know that the taste always works.
Serving suggestion: Hot with a liberal dollop of whipped cream.
M/A: Yes. This can be made up to 2 days in advance and heated in the oven or microwave.
* No

1	pound grated carrots—approximately (see "Notes")
1 ¹⁄₂	pints cold milk (I use whole, but 2% is good too)
1	teaspoon cardamom seeds
3	tablespoons unsalted butter
3 ¹⁄₂	tablespoons brown sugar
¹⁄₄	cup mixed unsalted whole pistachios/slivered almonds
¹⁄₈	cup raisins

- Put the milk, carrot, and cardamom seeds into a deep, non-stick pan. Bring to a boil and then simmer over medium heat and stir frequently with a wooden spoon to prevent sticking. Using the spoon, scrape any milk from the sides of the pan back into the pan before it burns. The carrots will soften, cook, and absorb the milk. After 50–55 minutes, the milk will have reduced, and there should be close to no sign of the liquid. In order to make the latter happen, turn the heat up if need be. Stir often—it may become tedious!

- Add the butter and brown the carrots for 10 minutes or so. Keep stirring.

- Add the sugar and brown for a further 10 minutes.

- Yes, keep stirring.

- Add the nuts and the raisins. Mix well for 5 minutes or so. Remove from the heat.

- It may be a bit mushy—no matter.

Done.

KHEER (RICE PUDDING)

Rice pudding is considered a comfort dish in any part of the world, and this recipe is certainly no exception. I include golden raisins to keep the colors light, and you will see that I choose for it to be on the stodgier side, but you can adapt your dried fruits and increase the amount of milk slightly to achieve your desired taste and consistency. Just right when snatched straight from the fridge.

Serves: 4–6
Preparation time: 5 minutes
Cooking time: 1 hour
Notes: If the pudding appears a little too thick for your liking, pour some heavy cream over it while serving—this will loosen it and bring an added richness to the plate. Try sliced dried apricots as an alternative to raisins.
Serving suggestion: All by itself.
M/A: Yes. I make a day in advance.
* No

2	pints cold milk (I use whole, but 2% is good too)
1	teaspoon cardamom seeds
¼	cup basmati rice, washed and drained
3	tablespoons packed brown sugar
2	tablespoons unsalted butter
¼	cup slivered, unsalted almonds
¼	cup golden raisins
	heavy/double/whipping cream (optional—see "Notes")

- Pour the milk and place the cardamom seeds in a deep, non-stick saucepan. Bring to boiling point over medium heat. Stir frequently with a wooden spoon to prevent sticking.

- Add the rice, sugar, and butter. Simmer over a low/medium flame. Stir at intervals—you may get weary but do not give up. The milk will begin to thicken. Using the spoon, scrape any milk from the sides of the pan back into the pan before it burns. After 45 minutes or so, the milk should reduce by about a third or a little more.

- Mix in the nuts and raisins.

- Taste test the milk and add more sugar if your taste requires it. Remove from the heat.

- Spoon into a serving dish or individual glasses, allow to fully cool (about 1 hour or so), then cover and refrigerate for 4–6 hours or overnight until chilled. (It may develop a surface skin—some love it, some spoon from beneath it.)

Done.

MEETHE CHAWAL (SWEET, SAFFRON RICE)

I still get nervous whenever I make this sweet rice because my mum's is always just right, and the whole world knows it—this dish is a testament to her kitchen skills. I am hoping that you will forget all jitters once you hear the compliments that come your way. This is a dessert that my family eats at "Raksha Bandhan." It is an annual occasion where a sister celebrates her sibling by tying a red, holy thread around her brother's wrist and feeding him some morsel of sweetness. The sister prays for her brother's well-being, success in life, and happiness. The brother returns the favor with a vow to look after his sister and a gift. I have no brothers but am blessed with many "cousin brothers"...I always reap enough English pounds to warrant more forceful prayers. I see it like this: my brothers' prosperity is my prosperity.

Serves: 6–8
Preparation time: 5 minutes + white rice (p. 114)
Cooking time: 20 minutes
Notes: Take the time to follow the preparation of the white rice (see "Rice" section) called for—also, please read the method below.
Use any dried fruits you like in the proportions that I suggest.
Serving suggestion: All by itself.
M/A: Yes. It heats up well in the microwave the next day—splash with cold water beforehand.
* No

	white rice (cooked as on p. 114—see method below before preparing this recipe), drained and cool
1	cup water
1/2	cup sugar
5	cloves
3"	cinnamon stick
1/2	teaspoon cardamom seeds
1/4	teaspoon saffron threads
2	tablespoons unsalted butter
1/2	cup unsalted, sliced almonds
1/4	cup unsalted pistachios
1/4	cup golden raisins
1/4	teaspoon yellow food coloring (optional)

- Make white rice as per recipe on p. 114 except that you should not add salt and that when the rice has been cooked for 9 minutes, remove the pan from the heat, uncover, fill the pot with cold tap water, pour off the water, refill with cold water, and drain the rice into a large sieve to stop any further cooking. Leave aside for at least 30 minutes. Phew!

- Meanwhile, in a small saucepan, bring 1 cup of water to a boil, add the sugar, cloves, cinnamon stick, cardamom seeds, saffron, and butter. Turn the heat to low and simmer the syrup for 3–4 minutes.

- Now put the syrup in a wide, shallow frying pan over a medium flame (pull out the cinnamon stick and cloves if you wish) and add the nuts and raisins. Heat through for about 2 minutes. Add the cool rice and the food coloring (if you opt for a brighter colored rice) and gently fold to allow all the grains to be coated with this sweetness. Turn the heat to low/medium and cover for 5 minutes. This will allow the rice to completely cook through.

- Remove the lid, stir gently once more to ensure that all the liquid has been absorbed, turn off the heat, re-cover, and leave for a further 10 minutes or until ready to eat.

- Uncover, fluff with a fork, and serve hot.

Done.

MEETHA POODA (SWEET PANCAKES)

These pancakes are served at breakfast time in Punjab. You see—we are all more alike than not. They are satisfying for a weekend morning but also pleasing as a sweet ending to a meal. Traditionally, they are prepared during the rainy season, and although far from India, Kargil often requests these as a snack when there is even the mere hint of a drizzle. I am most honored to oblige.

Serves: 4
Preparation time: 10 minutes
Cooking time: 10 minutes
Notes: You can substitute heavy/double/whipping cream for milk—a richer pancake.
Serving suggestion: I love to serve these poodas alongside Greek yogurt drizzled with agave syrup or honey—break off and dip. Kheer is a more traditional accompaniment (see "Desserts" section).
M/A: No
* No

1	cup whole-wheat atta flour
¼	cup brown sugar
1	teaspoon fennel seeds
½	teaspoon cardamom seeds
1 ½–2	cups milk (I use 2% or whole)
8	tablespoons canola oil
	powdered sugar (optional)
	Greek yogurt (optional)
	agave syrup (optional)

- Mix the first four ingredients in a deep bowl or jug, and gradually pour in the milk. Using a whisk, create a smooth but thick, pourable batter (judge the amount of milk needed to achieve this). Be sure to even out any lumps.

- Heat 1 tablespoon of oil in a non-stick frying pan. Keep the heat low when pouring and spreading the batter.

- Pour in about a quarter of the batter. Allow the pancake to grow to approximately 5" in diameter and ¼" thick by tilting the pan.

- Turn the heat to medium while cooking.

- After 2 minutes, drizzle a tablespoon of oil over the pancake and flip over. This prevents sticking.

- Cook the second side until golden brown too (a further 2–3 minutes).

- Remove from the pan, plate, and dust with powdered sugar. Repeat the above steps and take care to oil the pan and pancake when needed.

Done.

SEVIYAN (VERMICELLI)

This dish calls for vermicelli, a finer than spaghetti-like pasta that may be bought in long strands or circular clusters. It is also available in short lengths. I buy it from the Indian store in the nest shape I have described. A sweet pasta for dessert—yes, it works.

Serves: 6 if alongside ice cream
Preparation time: 5 minutes
Cooking time: 15 minutes
Notes: Leftovers do not heat well. You may use milk for an alternative version. The latter is preferable when a looser consistency is required—so 4 cups of milk (instead of 3 cups of cold water) would work.
Serving suggestion: Hot with vanilla ice cream.
M/A: No. However, you can prepare the syrup earlier and continue as below when you are ready to.
* No

3	cups cold water
¹⁄₃	cup brown sugar
¹⁄₄	teaspoon cardamom seeds
2″–3″	cinnamon stick
4	tablespoons unsalted butter
6	ounces vermicelli
	vanilla ice cream (optional)

- Place the first four ingredients into a pan and bring to the boil. Turn the heat to low, mix, and allow to simmer for 5 minutes. This will be your syrup.

- Meanwhile, melt the butter in another pan over low/medium heat and add the vermicelli nests (break up the long strands before adding) and keep stirring, using a wooden spoon. Gently turn and break up.

- Remove the cinnamon stick from the syrup and pour the syrup onto the pasta, combine well, cover, and allow to cook for 5 minutes over the same low/medium heat. Stir once during this time to check that the pasta is not sticking. If the pasta is catching the base of the pan, adjust the heat.

- Remove from the flame. Leave covered for a further 5 minutes.

- Serve hot with a scoop or two of vanilla ice cream.

Done.

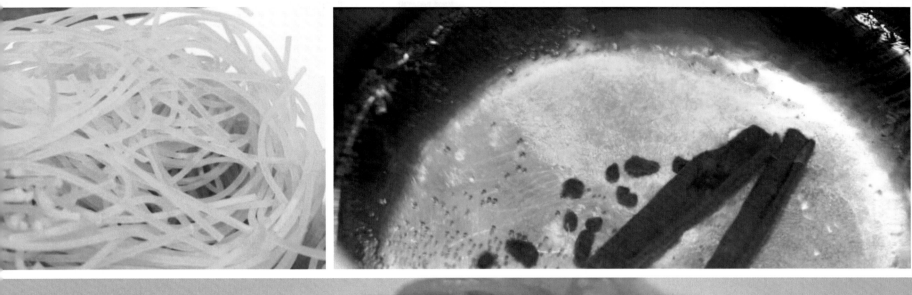

BANANAS FOSTER

This twist on the original Bananas Foster is sure to both surprise and delight. A dear friend of ours visited our home with the tempting offer of cooking dessert after dinner. I succumbed. Our friendship was permanently cemented...

Serves: 4
Preparation time: 3–5 minutes
Cooking time: 7–10 minutes
Notes: I looked at many readily available recipes for this dessert, and after testing and mixing up a few, I came up with this one—I must state that it is only the addition of cardamom that truly makes it mine.
Serving suggestion: Eat hot over vanilla ice cream.
M/A: No
* No

2	tablespoons unsalted butter
1/4	cup brown sugar
1/2	teaspoon cardamom seeds
1/4	cup dark rum
2	large bananas, sliced into 1/2″ rounds
	grated zest of an orange and vanilla ice cream for serving (optional)

- Melt the butter over medium heat in a shallow frying pan.

- Add the sugar and cardamom seeds, turn the heat to low, and stir for 2–3 minutes until the sugar dissolves.

- Put in the bananas and mix gently to cover both sides of the fruit. Try to keep the banana rounds intact.

- Add the rum, carefully ignite with a match (or it may alight on its own—be careful). You will see the flame die out after a minute or so.

- The contents of the pan will appear to be syrup-like but may not quite match the syrup that most of us picture. However, the flavor will be amazing—I promise you.

Done.

HALVA (SEMOLINA PUDDING)

Ownership of this dessert is claimed by the Turkish, the Middle Easterners, the North Africans, Jewish cuisine, and... yes...of course...us Indians. We eat halva on religious occasions in particular—namely a god's birthday...that was the excuse anyway. I remember pondering why Lord Krishna had already celebrated two birthdays that year when my mum would give us yet another heavenly helping. It is always served at the Hindu temple as "prasad" (a blessed food offering from the gods). Buttery, sugary, nutty, and fruity. Divine.

Serves: 6
Preparation time: 10 minutes
Cooking time: 40–45 minutes
Notes: Growing up, I detested the raisins in the halva, so I often totally leave out the fruit, or I increase the amount of nuts to ¹/₂ cup (or I just spoon the raisins into my children's bowls).
Serving suggestion: All by itself or with pooris (see "Breads" section).
M/A: Best when eaten immediately. However, this heats perfectly in the microwave the following day.
* No

3 ¹/₂	cups cold water
1 ¹/₄	cup packed brown sugar
1	teaspoon cardamom seeds
8	tablespoons unsalted butter
1	cup semolina flour ("suji"/"sooji")

<u>dried fruit:</u> (optional—see "Notes")

¹/₄	cup golden raisins
¹/₄	cup slivered almonds/unsalted pistachio nuts

- In a small pan, make a syrup by boiling and stirring together the water, sugar, and cardamom seeds for 30 seconds or so. Then allow the liquid to simmer over the lowest heat until you are ready for it. Stir from time to time to prevent the sugar from burning—you will want the sugar to dissolve. (You should lose about a ¹/₂ cup of liquid due to evaporation during the time it takes you to carry out the following steps and until the syrup is needed.)

- Meanwhile, melt the butter in another non-stick pan over a low/medium flame.

- Add the semolina flour, turn the heat to medium, stir with a wooden spoon, and cook the flour for about 20–25 minutes. Mix the flour almost continuously so that it does not burn. You will notice the semolina change color from a creamish shade to that of the cleanest, golden sand that you can imagine. A rich, buttery scent should surround you—my mum says it is this aroma that signals that the flour is cooking.

- Stir in the raisins and the nuts. Then, taking care...it may spit...pour in the syrup. Bring the contents of the pan to a vigorous boil, mix, and then immediately bring to a low heat. Cover and leave untouched for 10 minutes.

- After 10 minutes, switch off the heat and leave covered for a further 10 minutes.

- Serve hot.

Done.

MANGO KULFI (ICE CREAM)

Well, all that I can say is that I challenge you to eat just one. I often make my kulfis ample enough for two to share (or battle out!). Ridiculously delicious.

Serves: 6–8 (it depends upon the mold size)
Preparation time: 5 minutes
Cooking time: 20–25 minutes
Notes: This lasts for up to 2 weeks in the freezer—it tends to develop ice crystals after that. I am sure there are tricks to be learned with an ice cream maker, etc., but I have not the patience nor the equipment.
Having said that, if I do ever invest in an ice cream maker, I will have no problem in justifying its purchase.
If you do not have any mangoes, just omit from the recipe and call it a pistachio kulfi instead.
Serving suggestion: All by itself.
M/A: Yes
* Yes

1	can evaporated milk—approximately 12 ounces
¹/₂	teaspoon cardamom seeds
2"–3"	cinnamon stick
2	tablespoons ground almonds
¹/₃	cup unsalted pistachios, coarsely chopped
1	can condensed milk—approximately 14 ounces
1	cup heavy/double/whipping cream
2–3	mangoes, pulp only (mushed and whizzed in a blender until smooth) **OR** 1 cup mango pulp (canned from the Indian/ethnic store)

- Pour the evaporated milk into a non-stick saucepan, add the cardamom seeds and a 2"–3" cinnamon stick, and allow to simmer over low/medium heat for 10–15 minutes or so. Stir to prevent sticking and adjust the heat as needed. The spices will infuse the milk. Remove from the heat. Strain if you like. I do not. I just scoop out the cinnamon stick and leave in the seeds because I like the crunch.

- Add the ground almonds and pistachios.

- Meanwhile, in a bowl whisk together the condensed milk, heavy cream, and mango pulp.

- Now, combine the contents of the pan with those of the bowl.

- Pour into ice cream molds or freezer-safe glass dishes. Using a spoon, try to distribute the nuts evenly—you do not want one guest to have all the bonuses. Cover and freeze until hard...about 6 hours.

- Before serving, remove the lid and dip the dish or mold (all the way up to the rim) into a bowl/bath of boiling water for 10–15 seconds. This will loosen the kulfi and allow it to slide out somewhat elegantly.

Done.

CHILI, CHOCOLATE SAUCE

Sweet and savory desserts are all the rage. (Have you come across bacon and maple syrup or chipotle and black bean cupcakes yet?) Anyway, my sister is a chocolate-lover and suggested that I attempt this coupling. There was no real attempt made—it is so very easy. If cautious, turn the heat up gradually by adding the spice a little at a time and tasting it as you go along. I guess how daring you are is just a matter of who is joining you for dinner...

Serves: It will be enough to drizzle over 20–24 cupcakes or multiple cookies.
Preparation time: 2 minutes
Cooking time: 15 minutes
Notes: Use the chocolate of your choice—no hard rules for this recipe.
Serving suggestion: Try dipping strawberries and bananas into the sauce for a surprising fondue or spoon over a warm croissant at breakfast time.
M/A: Yes. Just heat through, very gently, before serving.
* No

1	cup dark chocolate chips (I use mildly sweet ones but you choose what you like)
1	cup heavy/double/whipping cream
1 1/2	teaspoons dried chili flakes
1	fresh, red chili—seeds and membranes discarded, chopped (leave a little for garnishing)
	a little desiccated coconut for decorating (optional)

- Put the chocolate into a non-stick pan, and over very low heat allow to melt. Stir with a wooden spoon to prevent burning. (I never really bother with water baths for chocolate anymore, so just watch the heat under your saucepan and you will be fine.)

- Pour in the cream. Continue to stir to create a smooth sauce. Heat through thoroughly. This will take about 10 minutes.

- Mix in the chili flakes and fresh chili.

- While it is still hot, drizzle the chocolate sauce over the cupcakes or shortbread and allow to cool. This is the time to sprinkle on the coconut if you so choose and garnish with fresh or dried chili if you fancy.

Done.

DRINKS...

MASALA CHAI (SPICED TEA)

"A cup of tea?"—growing up in England, my ears invited the rhetorical question several times a day. A cup of chai will warm the welcome for a guest, soothe an ache, digest a bite, and seemingly (even if only for a short while) determine everything to be okay. Indians have no fewer problems (or frayed nerves) and therefore consume as much tea as the British. It is often ladled into a thick glass by a roadside vendor, and the sound of slurping the steaming tea is not only acceptable but quite desirable as it enhances the cure-all, therapeutic benefits of this tonic.

Not sure if I should divulge, but I revel in the risk of successfully sneaking a flask of masala chai into the Bollywood movie cinema here in Atlanta—if I buy a concession-stand samosa, then surely my hidden but forbidden beverage is somehow permissible?

Serves: 3–4
Preparation time: 2 minutes
Cooking time: 10 minutes (approximately)
Notes: Choose the spices and herbs that speak to you (see "Spices and Herbs" section). I have offered suggestions, but you can build your tea as you wish. My favorite is the ginger and black pepper. Sample some combinations and adjust the measurements to your liking—you will discover a favorite or at least begin to understand what your mood calls for.
I never use loose-leaf tea because the tea bags that I grew up with are available here in Atlanta. I use "PG Tips"—a British blend of Assam, Ceylon, and Kenyan teas. Black tea is my choice.
Serving suggestion: I appreciate this drink after a meal or with a spicy appetizer at teatime.
M/A: No
* No

5	cups cold water
Possibilities (choose 2–3 ingredients from this list):	
¹/₂	teaspoon ginger powder **OR** 1 teaspoon freshly grated ginger
¹/₄	teaspoon black pepper
1″	cinnamon stick
2–3	green cardamom pods (cracked open)
1	black cardamom pod (cracked open)
2–3	cloves
¹/₂	teaspoon fennel seeds
¹/₄	teaspoon carom seeds
2	tea bags (see "Notes")
1	cup milk (I use 2%, but whatever you have will work)
	sugar to taste (optional)

- Pour the water into a pan, add the 2–3 ingredients that you chose from the list above, and bring to a boil over a medium/high flame. Allow the contents of the pan to boil vigorously for a minute or so.

- Add the tea bags and continue to boil for 30 seconds and then decrease the heat to low/medium for a further minute.

- Pour in the milk, allow the tea to simmer for about 2 minutes, then bring to a boil for a few seconds (do not allow it to boil over), and remove from the flame.

- Strain into the drinking vessel of your choice. Stir in sugar to taste.

Done.

ICED, MASALA CHAI (ICED, SPICED TEA)

Make the masala chai (as on the previous page), remove from the heat, and allow to cool. Next, pour into a jug and refrigerate for 2–3 hours. Serve over ice—not traditionally Indian, but a refreshing alternative to an iced tea. If you prefer a non-dairy version, simply omit the milk and add an extra cup of water to the original recipe. For a more milky drink, increase the milk-to-water ratio.

BADAAM MILK (ALMOND MILK)

Custom dictates that the Indian groom drinks this warm, sugary, cardamom-laced concoction on his wedding night—there is no doubt in the minds of all "who know" that his bride will be thankful for her tender, dutiful, and oh so efficacious spouse.

Serves: 3–4
Preparation time: 10 minutes
Cooking time: 10 minutes (approximately)
Notes: In addition to kicking off the honeymoon, this milk is often prepared in order to break a fast or as a celebratory drink on religious occasions.
Do not serve a large helping as it is quite filling and sweet too.
No need to peel the almonds.
Serving suggestion: As a snack or great alongside break-fast.
I have served a tasting in shot glasses at a brunch.
M/A: Yes, if serving chilled. Make up to 1 day ahead.
* No

4	cups milk (I use 2% or whole)
3	tablespoons sugar
¹/₂	teaspoon cardamom seeds
¹/₂	teaspoon fennel seeds

- In a pan, bring to a boil the above ingredients for 30 seconds or so, and then lower the heat and simmer for 5 minutes (take care not to allow it to boil over). Stir once or twice.

- Mix in **2 tablespoons ground almonds** and **2 table-spoons ground pistachio nuts**. Simmer for a further 2 minutes.

- Drink hot or remove from the heat and allow to cool. Pour into a jug and refrigerate for 2–3 hours or overnight. Stir to distribute the nuts and serve chilled.

- Garnish with **ground pistachios (optional)**.

Done.

MANGO LASSI
(YOGURT-BASED MANGO DRINK)

Lassi (the Punjabi smoothie) is traditionally taken in the farming regions of Northern India by agricultural workers begging for some cool relief from the often grueling summer sun. It does not necessarily include fruit—sugar or salt to taste are alternative options (see the following recipes).

Serves: 4
Preparation time: 5 minutes
Cooking time: N/A
Notes: Frozen mangoes will work.
Serving suggestion: As a snack or great alongside breakfast.
I have served a tasting in shot glasses at a brunch.
M/A: No
* No

2	ripe mangoes (peeled, flesh removed, and chopped)
2	cups plain yogurt (low-fat works)
	ice cubes (approximately 1 cup)
	sugar to taste (3 tablespoons approximately— depends upon sweetness of the mangoes)
¹/₂	cup cold water (approximately) to help with the consistency

Place the above ingredients in a blender. Whiz together until smooth. Test for sugar and consistency (adjust with more sugar or water if required). Serve straight away.

Done.

LASSI
(YOGURT-BASED DRINK)

This is so a "scorching-day-in-the-garden" kind of drink. Newcastle is not known for too many of those days, but my mum would run to retrieve the blender when there was even a glimmer of the sun...Now I check my weather app and rush to do the very same...

Serves: 4
Preparation time: 5 minutes
Cooking time: N/A
Notes: Most prefer one or the other. Try them both. Are you sweet or savory?
Serving suggestion: At brunch.
M/A: No
* No

Savory lassi:
2	cups plain yogurt (low-fat works)
	ice cubes (approximately 1 cup)
1/2	teaspoon salt
1/2	teaspoon black pepper (extra for garnish— optional)
1	cup cold water
1/2	teaspoon ground cumin (optional)
	a handful of cilantro, chopped (optional)
8–10	mint leaves, chopped (optional)

Sweet lassi:
2	cups plain yogurt (low-fat works)
	ice cubes (approximately 1 cup)
1	cup cold water
3	tablespoons sugar

Place the ingredients for either recipe in a blender. Whiz together until smooth. Test for salt/pepper (savory) or sugar (sweet) and adjust accordingly. Serve straight away.

Done.

LYCHEE MARTINI

Shake **2 parts vodka**, **3 parts lychee juice** (available at the Indian grocery store), and **a generous splash of club soda**. Pour over **crushed ice** and garnish with **a lychee** (use canned lychees from the Indian store when you cannot get your hands on fresh ones).

Done.

The mere reference to a martini prompts me to when I first moved to Atlanta. I was at a happening bar amongst a young and lively gathering of new(ish) friends and was suddenly conscious of the fact that while the others were pointing to "Cosmopolitan" and "Manhattan" cocktails on the menu, my drink order would not appear trendy or cool enough. On the spur of the moment, I found myself confidently demanding a "dry martini."

My husband politely and secretly mouthed, "Are you sure?" in my direction. How dare he? What if someone had witnessed this embarrassing interaction? I quickly raised my hand and added that I always have extra olives.

My glamorous glass made its appearance. It was all mine.

I tried not to make eye contact as my throat burned horribly. I scrubbed my lips to erase as much aftertaste as I could. Somehow, my husband magically produced an orange juice and stirred a little into my big mistake.

Home, much earlier than I had expected, I rang and awoke my dad in the wee English hours...urgently, I demanded, "Dad, what did you put in those martinis that you used to make on Friday nights for Geetu and I?"

"7 UP, a grape, and a paper umbrella, Rad," he yawned.

Persistence possibly pays...lately, I have been spotted exuding poise and worldliness while sipping on a very, very dirty martini—no one even notices me merrily licking my lips...

POMEGRANATE GIMLET

Shake **2 parts gin**, **3 parts pomegranate juice**, and **a generous splash of club soda**. Pour over **crushed ice** and add **a squeeze of orange** or **lime** (whatever you happen to have in your fruit bowl).

Done.

Although not Indian in origin, per se, I encountered this cocktail at a NYC Indian restaurant. It has sadly since closed its doors, but I continue to reminisce over this refreshing aperitif. An award-winning opening to any spiced dish on the menu and a most congenial means of ensuring one's daily dose of antioxidants. Cheers!

A NOTE BEFORE WE CLOSE...

I have endeavored to create and to tell you my story. In order to do so, I have punctuated with ingredients, recipes, images, and memories that speak to me.

It is often voiced that the process of creativity is not complete until it is shared.

My hope is that sharing something that is meaningful to me has inspired something that is meaningful to you...

INDEX

ABOUT THE AUTHOR...

Radhika Behl grew up in Newcastle upon Tyne, England. Her mother, grandmother, and aunties collectively (and quite intentionally) invested in her their knowledge of Indian culture, customs, and cuisine. However it came about, the passion to taste and meddle in the kitchen was born. The circle continues...Radhika, too, felt the urge and maternal calling to become the "imparter" of wisdom. In this, her first cookbook, she shares her memories, her heritage, and the recipes that have nourished her childhood and now nurture her own home.

Although Radhika secretly yearns to be described as crafty and creative, athletic, a yogi, and an avid reader—she has accepted that this is going to be her long-term goal. With her husband and their two children, she feels blessed to be living in Atlanta, Georgia. Radhika is her true self whilst teaching pre-k and the occasional Indian cooking class. She most appreciates "car talk" (both silly and spiritual) on the morning drives to school, family travels, dining with friends, and the magic of falling-out and making-up over memorable mouthfuls at the kitchen table.

My parents and just a small handful of my aunties and uncles...they arrived from India and labored to remain true to their roots while molding themselves and forging Newcastle, England, in a way that would become their work, their community, their family, their home—their new life. In doing so, they shaped the UK to be all of that and beyond for the children who stayed and for those who moved away but will forever know it as "home, home."

They are the reasons for my awaited returns to England and are faithfully and tirelessly the answers to many of my own choices at "home" today...